THE EXPO 86™ COOKBOOK

by Susan Mendelson
food photography by Derik Murray

EXPO SOUVENIRS / WHITECAP BOOKS

Other Books by Susan Mendelson:

Mama Never Cooked Like This (Vancouver: Talonbooks, 1980)
Let Me in the Kitchen (Vancouver/Toronto: Douglas & McIntyre, 1982)
Nuts About Chocolate — with Deborah Roitberg (Vancouver/Toronto, Douglas &
    McIntyre, 1983)
Fresh Tarts — with Deborah Roitberg (Vancouver/Toronto, Douglas & McIntyre, 1985)

Copyright page:

copyright © 1986 Susan Mendelson

Expo Souvenirs
A Division of Specialty Mfg. Ltd.
1052 Homer Street
Vancouver, B.C.
V6B 2W9 Canada

Whitecap Books
1086 West 3rd Street
North Vancouver, B.C.
V7P 3J6 Canada

Editors: Marilyn Sacks and David Robinson
Cover and food photographs: Derik Murray
Book design: David Robinson
Typesetting, printing and binding: D.W. Friesen & Sons

Printed and bound in Canada.

First printing: March 1986

Canadian Cataloguing in Publication Data

  Mendelson, Susan, 1952–
    The Expo '86 cookbook

  Includes index.
  ISBN 0–920620–85–X

  1. Cookery. I. Title.
  TX715.M45 1986   641.5   C86–091030–X

Contents

Introduction / *9*

Hot & Cold Hors d'Oeuvres / *11*

Salads / *23*

Quiche & Pizza / *32*

Chicken / *44*

Fish & Seafood / *50*

Beef & Veal / *66*

Casseroles, Vegetable Side Dishes & Rice / *70*

Restaurant Favourites / *77*

Sweets & Treats / *105*

Breads & Muffins / *120*

Acknowledgements / *123*

Index / *125*

Introduction

Vancouver is a city that generates feelings of joy in its visitors and inhabitants alike. Its picturesque setting, coastal location and mild climate are the ingredients of a lifestyle that emphasizes the pleasures of outdoor activity. The clichéed Vancouverite skies Grouse Mountain in the morning and gets in a quick game of tennis at Stanley Park before noon, so that he will have time for a round of golf in the afternoon. Certainly the proximity of the mountains and the sea provides many delightful diversions for those who live here.

From this lifestyle, with its emphasis on leisure and health, comes a corresponding style of eating and entertaining. Just as the sixties health food craze started on the West Coast, so have many recent food trends that you now find in large metropolitan centres every–where. The emphasis on food in Vancouver is on simplicity, lightness and freshness. This is reflected in the fresh salads and fish dishes that are served in our restaurants and homes. Diversity and sophistication are also stressed. Hot and cold hors d'oeuvres offered at most Vancouver parties now allow the diner to taste a little of everything — all without breaking the budget. Specialty food stores can be found in increasing numbers, reminding Vancouverites of the city's varied ethnic make-up; and burgeoning produce markets keep us supplied with fresh fruit and vegetables from around the world.

Lest you think that all those joggers, swimmers, cyclists and skiers are mere fitness fiends, we hasten to confess that many of us indulge in exercise because we are haunted by a craving for sweets — desserts that have more chocolate, that are gooier and richer than anything you've experienced anywhere else! (Don't forget, Nanaimo Bars are a West Coast invention!) And remember, most of these recipes in this book are a lot easier to prepare than you would think. Otherwise, how would so many of us find the time to be out there running, swimming or skiing?

With these recipes — some of our best — we invite the world to share our cuisine. We hope that when you eat our food in your part of the world, you will remember Vancouver with special affection!

Susan Mendelson,
Vancouver, B.C.
March, 1986.

Hot & Cold Hors d' Oeuvres

COCONUT SCALLOPS

1 lb. fresh scallops	Rinse and drain well.

Marinade:

1/4 cup fresh lemon juice 2 Tbsp. fresh lime juice 2 tsp. curry powder 1/2 tsp. powdered ginger 1/2 tsp. salt	Mix ingredients well and pour over scallops in a glass bowl. Marinate 2 hours.
	Drain scallops, reserving marinade.

Batter:

2 cups flour 2 tsp. baking powder	Sift together.
1 1/3 cups cold milk	Add and combine.
Reserved marinade	Add and combine. Dip scallops in batter and shake off excess.
1 1/2 cups long threaded coconut	Roll in coconut.
Vegetable oil for deep frying	Heat oil in deep skillet or deep fryer at 350°F–375°F. Add scallops and fry until golden.

This recipe is also fantastic made with B.C. prawns! *Serves 6–8.*

EASY BRIE & PECANS IN PHYLLO

Preheat oven to 400°F.

1 lb. Brie	Cut cheese into 24 small pieces.
1/2 lb. phyllo pastry	Cut sheets, one at a time, into 11″ × 3″ strips.
1/2 cup melted butter	Brush each strip with butter.
1/2 cup chopped pecans	Sprinkle strips with nuts.

Place a piece of Brie at the bottom right-hand corner of each pastry strip and form a triangle by folding the corner up to meet the opposite side, enclosing the cheese. Continue to fold the pastry in a series of diagonals, making sure that the dough is well sealed with each turn. (If not well sealed, Brie may ooze out as it melts.) Place on a cookie sheet and bake 16–18 minutes until golden.

Makes 4 dozen.

CARAMEL ALMOND BRIE

Preheat oven to 375°F.

3 egg whites 2 Tbsp. sugar	Mix together.
2 cups flaked almonds, toasted	Stir in almonds. Set aside.
2-lb. round of Brie (or Camembert)	Place cheese on ungreased baking sheet.
3 egg yolks	Brush yolks over top and sides of cheese.
	Press nut mixture into top and sides.

Bake 20 minutes. Let cool 10 minutes. Top with glaze.

Caramel Glaze:

2 cups sugar 3/4 cup water 1 tsp. lemon juice	Combine and bring to a boil. Let boil for about 15 minutes until a dark amber colour. Pour over Brie.
	Let stand 30 minutes before serving.

Your guests will never believe how easy this impressive presentation is to make.
Serves 12–15.

FRIED BRIE

1 1/2 lbs. Brie, well chilled	Cut into 1" squares.
1/4 cup flour	Sprinkle over bottom of flat dish.
2 eggs, beaten 3 Tbsp. chopped fresh parsley 2 Tbsp. light oil Freshly ground pepper Dash of hot pepper sauce	Combine in bowl.
2 1/2 cups fine bread crumbs 1/2 cup sesame seeds	Mix together and spread in separate dish.
	Roll cheese squares in flour, dip in egg mixture, roll in crumbs. Place on cookie sheet and freeze 35–45 minutes until firm.
Vegetable oil for deep frying	Heat oil in deep skillet or deep fryer at 350°F–375°F. Add cheese a few squares at a time (leaving rest in freezer until ready to cook) and fry until crisp (about 2 minutes).
	Drain on paper towels and serve at once with fresh baguette and raspberry or blackberry preserves.

Makes about 2 dozen.

CAMEMBERT-EN-CROÛTE

This croûte can be made in different sizes, depending on the number of people you wish to serve.

1/4 lb. of puff pastry 5-oz. wheel of Camembert	*Serves 3–4.*
10 oz. frozen puff pastry 2-lb. wheel of Camembert	*Serves 12–15.*
2 lbs. puff pastry 5-lb. wheel of Camembert (or Brie)	*Serves 35 or more.*

To prepare:

Puff pastry	On lightly floured board, roll out pastry until it is 1″ larger than round of cheese.
Camembert (or Brie)	Place cheese on pastry.
1 egg, beaten	Brush pastry around cheese with egg wash. Top with a larger round of pastry. With small paring knife or kitchen shears, cut top pastry to meet bottom pastry evenly.
	Crimp bottom and top crusts by pressing together. Use excess pastry pieces to decorate croûte. Brush with egg wash.
	Bake at 400°F until outside is puffy, crisp and golden brown: 15 minutes for 5-oz. wheel; 20–22 minutes for 2-lb. wheel; 25–30 minutes for 5-lb. wheel.

Check occasionally while baking to make sure the cheese does not seep out. If it does, remove croûte from oven. Let the cheese sit until almost firm, then cut off part of the top, scoop the cheese back in and replace the top. Your guests will never know and your party will be rescued.

Variations: Try topping the cheese with fresh blueberries and a sprinkling of sugar before covering with the crust. A sprinkling of brown sugar and toasted pecans also make a delicious topping for the cheese. Have fun experimenting with this recipe.

SESAME, POPPY & CHEESE STRAWS

Preheat oven to 375°F.

Sesame Straws:

10 oz. frozen puff pastry	Roll out pastry to make a large rectangle about 1/2" thick.
1/2 cup sesame seeds 1/4 cup grated Parmesan cheese }	Sprinkle on pastry. Use a rolling pin to press seeds and cheese into pastry.
	Cut into 1" × 3" strips and twist into corkscrew shapes. Place on a cookie sheet and bake 15 minutes until golden brown.

Poppy Seed Straws:

Follow above instructions, substituting 1/2 cup poppy seeds.

Cheddar Cheese Straws:

10 oz. frozen puff pastry	Roll out pastry.
2 cups Cheddar cheese 1/2 cup Parmesan cheese	Grate cheeses and set aside.
2 eggs 2 Tbsp. light cream }	Beat together and brush onto dough.
	Sprinkle cheese over dough, pressing in with rolling pin or hands.
	Cut, twist and bake as above.

Serve hot or cold as a crispy snack with hors d'oeuvres or with lunch. *Makes 3 dozen.*

BOCCONCINI

2 lbs. fresh whole-milk Mozzarella	Cut into 1" squares.
1 cup olive oil 1 tsp. dried hot peppers 1 tsp. dried oregano 2 Tbsp. minced fresh parsley }	Mix together. Marinate cheese in dressing for 6–8 hours. Serve with crackers.

Originally made with fresh buffalo milk, Bocconcini introduces us to the new taste and texture of fresh Mozzarella. You can also toss Bocconcini with raw and/or lightly cooked vegetables and serve on lettuce for a luncheon dish. *Serves 12–15.*

MARINATED MOZZARELLA

1 lb. fresh whole-milk Mozzarella

Slice and arrange on a shallow dish.

4 Tbsp. extra virgin olive oil
3 Tbsp. vegetable oil
2 Tbsp. minced sundried tomatoes
2 tsp. dried chili peppers
1 tsp. red pepper flakes
1/2 tsp. minced garlic
2 Tbsp. minced fresh parsley or
2 Tbsp. minced fresh basil

Mix thoroughly and pour over Mozzarella slices. Let sit at room temperature 3–4 hours.

This Mozzarella is not to be confused with the cheese you buy to grate over pizza. Look for it in specialty cheese stores or in Italian import food stores. Extra virgin olive oil comes from the first pressing of the olives and is the purest olive oil you can buy. You can find it in gourmet food shops. Garnish Marinated Mozzarella with fresh parsley or basil leaves. Serve with fresh baguette slices and, for extra colour, sliced tomatoes. *Serves 4.*

HERB & GARLIC CHEESE

2 cups cream cheese
2 cloves garlic, crushed
2 Tbsp. pesto (*see p. 17*)
3 Tbsp. finely chopped fresh parsley
1 tsp. chopped fresh thyme or
1/2 tsp. dried thyme
2 tsp. chopped fresh basil or
1 tsp. dried basil
Freshly ground pepper
(the more the better)

Using food processor, electric mixer or elbow grease, combine until all ingredients are well blended.

Serve this tangy cheese on Melba toast, or spoon it into a mould and let your guests spread it on crackers or baguette slices. *Serves 10–12.*

PESTO

3 cups fresh basil
1 cup fresh parsley
1/2 cup pine nuts, toasted
4 cloves garlic, crushed
1/2 cup grated Parmesan cheese

Using blender or on/off position of food processor, process until well blended.

1 cup virgin olive oil

Add oil gradually, continuing to process until a creamy paste is formed.

1/2 tsp. freshly ground pepper
Salt to taste

Add seasonings.

Pesto is a marvellous addition to soups and sauces, and it freezes well. When fresh basil is available, make extra for future use. I felt that I had discovered a new world when I discovered pesto. I hope you love it too!

FAMOUS LAZY GOURMET CAVIAR PIE

9" quiche pan or pie plate

2 ripe avocados

Mash in pan or plate.

2 Tbsp. finely chopped red onion

Sprinkle avocado with onion.

6 hardboiled eggs, grated
3 Tbsp. mayonnaise

Mix together gently and spread carefully over avocado.

4-oz. jar lumpfish caviar

Using a small spoon and a light touch, spread caviar over top of pie.

Serve with sesame crackers or baguette slices.

This elegant creation was introduced to Vancouver in 1979; it's now standard fare at most hors d'oeuvres buffets. *Serves 12–15.*

LAZY GOURMET LOX MOUSSE

1 lb. whipped cream cheese
2 tsp. lemon juice
3–4 oz. smoked salmon (lox)
Freshly ground pepper to taste

In a food processor or an electric mixer, puree until well blended.

Take home our B.C. smoked salmon, keep it up to one year in your freezer and enjoy the flavours of Vancouver year round. Serve on bagels, pumpernickel or sesame crackers. *Serves 10 as an hors d'oeuvre.*

DEEP-FRIED ZUCCHINI STICKS

2 medium-sized zucchini 1/2 tsp. salt	Cut zucchini into 2 1/2" × 3" strips. Toss with salt and let sit 10 minutes, then pat dry with paper towel.
3/4 cup flour Freshly ground pepper	Dredge sticks with seasoned flour.
2 medium-sized eggs 1 tsp. Dijon mustard 2 dashes hot pepper sauce	Beat together. Dip zucchini sticks in egg mixture and let excess drip off.
1 3/4 cups fine dried bread crumbs	Roll zucchini in crumbs.
Vegetable oil for frying	Heat 1" oil in deep skillet or deep fryer to 375°F. Fry zucchini in small batches for about 2 minutes until brown and crisp. Keep warm in 250°F oven.
	Serve warm with Spicy Mustard Sauce.

Spicy Mustard Sauce:

1/4 cup Dijon mustard 1 tsp. dry mustard 3 Tbsp. sugar 2 Tbsp. fresh lemon juice 1/2 cup mayonnaise 2 dashes hot pepper sauce 2 Tbsp. chopped fresh dill (*optional*)	Whisk together until well blended.

For extra texture and flavour, try a combination of cornflake crumbs, matzoh meal or wheat germ with the bread crumbs. *Makes 3–4 dozen.*

RATATOUILLE TARTS

1/2 cup olive oil 4 cloves garlic, crushed 1 large onion, chopped 2 leeks, sliced (white part only)	Heat oil and sauté garlic, onion and leeks until transparent.
1 medium eggplant 2 small zucchini	Dice the eggplant and zucchini into very small pieces and add to above.
1 red bell pepper, chopped 6 ripe tomatoes	Chop the tomatoes into very small pieces and add with pepper to above.
1/4 cup tomato paste 2 Tbsp. chopped fresh basil or 2 tsp. dried basil Salt and freshly ground pepper to taste	Add paste and seasonings and simmer uncovered 1 hour until mixture is thick.
2 tsp. capers	Add during last 15 minutes of cooking.
Pastry crust (*see p. 36*)	Roll out pastry to make 48 – 2″ tarts. Bake at 350°F for 12 minutes.
	Fill baked shells with ratatouille mixture.
1/4 cup grated Parmesan cheese	Sprinkle tarts with cheese. Bake at 350°F for 10 minutes until tarts are just warm and cheese is melted.

These tarts appear everywhere in the south of France from 2″ and 3″ minis to large flans and now have been adopted by West Coast caterers.

ROQUEFORT-WALNUT WON TONS

1/2 lb. won ton wrappers

| 8 oz. cream cheese 3 oz. Roquefort cheese 1 cup chopped walnuts | Mix together thoroughly. Drop by 1/2 tsp. onto centre of wrappers. |

| 2 eggs 1 Tbsp. water | Brush egg wash on wrapper around cheese. Bring edges of won ton together and press to seal. (The top will look a little like an unopened flower.) Be sure won tons are well sealed. |

| Vegetable oil | Heat 2″ of oil in large skillet. Add won tons and deep fry 3–4 minutes until crisp and brown. Serve warm. |

Everyone falls in love with this combination French and Chinese hors d'oeuvre. You can make them ahead of time and simply reheat for 5 minutes on a baking sheet in a 350°F oven. *Makes 4–5 dozen.*

GRAVLAX

5-lb. fresh sockeye or red spring salmon, filleted with skin on, but with all bones removed

| 1/4 cup coarse salt 1/4 cup sugar 3 Tbsp. white peppercorns, coarsely ground 2 large bunches fresh dill, chopped | In a glass pyrex dish, place half of salmon, skin side down. Cover with seasonings. Place other half of salmon on top, skin side up. |

Cover dish with plastic wrap. Put weight on top of salmon. Refrigerate 3–4 days, turning the salmon once every day.

Marvellous for Sunday brunch served with Mustard Sauce (*see pp. 62 or 63*) or Cucumber Dill Sauce (*see p. 61*). *Serves up to 20 as an hors d'oeuvre.*

Photo #1: Gravlax.

Salads

FRENCH POTATO SALAD

14 small new red potatoes, scrubbed

In medium-sized saucepan, boil until just tender (about 20 minutes). Drain, cut in halves and let cool 5 minutes.

3 Tbsp. chopped fresh parsley
2 Tbsp. fresh dill or
2 tsp. dried dill
6 Tbsp. chopped green onions
4 Tbsp. finely chopped red onion
1 large red pepper, chopped (*optional*)

Combine with potatoes.

Dressing:

1/3 cup red wine vinegar
3/4 cup olive oil
2 tsp. Dijon mustard
1 clove garlic, crushed
Black pepper, liberally ground

Mix well together and toss with potatoes while still warm.

A light, fresh salad with a tangy vinaigrette dressing — delicious hot or cold. *Serves 6.*

Photo #2 (*clockwise from left*): Sticky Cinnamon Buns, L.G. Bars, Triple Chunk Cookies and Brie–en–Croûte (atop strawberry plate), Tomatoes with Pesto Vinaigrette, Pasta Pesto Salad, Crispy Chicken and French Potato Salad (*at left on plate*).

NEW POTATO SALAD

16 small new red potatoes,
scrubbed clean
3 hardboiled eggs
4 medium–sized green onions,
white part and 1″ of green, chopped
4 Tbsp. chopped fresh parsley
10-oz. jar artichoke hearts

Combine in bowl.

1/2 cup sour cream
3/4 cup mayonnaise
2 Tbsp. Dijon mustard
1/2 tsp. salt

Whisk together, then toss gently with above.

Refrigerate 4–6 hours to allow flavours to blend.

This is best served with the freshest new potatoes. Take in a picnic to English Bay!
Serves 6–8.

TAMARI-GINGER MARINATED VEGETABLES

1 cup chopped broccoli (large pieces)
1 cup chopped cauliflower
1 cup snow peas

Blanch in boiling water for 1 minute, then refresh under cold running water until cold.

1 red bell pepper, sliced
1/2 cup chopped red onion
1 cup small mushroom caps or
large mushrooms, sliced
3/4 cup chopped carrots

Combine with above in large bowl.

Soy-Ginger Marinade:

4 Tbsp. red wine vinegar
2 Tbsp. Tamari
or
soy sauce
1 clove garlic, crushed
2 tsp. grated fresh ginger or
1/2 tsp. powdered ginger
1 tsp. sugar

In separate bowl, combine ingredients in this order.

3/4 cup light vegetable oil
2–3 drops of sesame oil (*optional*)

Gradually beat in vegetable oil, adding sesame oil, if desired.

Cover vegetables with marinade and let sit at least 1 hour, tossing occasionally.

4 Tbsp. sesame seeds, toasted

Sprinkle over salad before serving.

This salad can marinate overnight. Everyone loves the marinade. Feel free to use it as a salad dressing. *Serves 6–8.*

TRIPLE PEPPER SALAD WITH GARLIC

2 large red bell peppers 1 large green bell pepper 2 large yellow bell peppers	Char peppers over open flame or under broiler until skins are blackened on all sides. Remove from heat. Place in a paper bag and let steam 10 minutes. Peel, core and remove seeds, saving any juices. Rinse peppers and pat dry.
	Cut into 2″ strips and arrange on a platter. Sprinkle with the juices.
2 Tbsp. balsamic vinegar Freshly ground pepper to taste	Whisk vinegar and pepper together.
1/3–1/2 cup extra virgin olive oil	Slowly add oil until blended in.
2–3 cloves garlic, crushed	Stir in garlic.
	Pour dressing over peppers, stirring to coat well.

Balsamic vinegar is a well-aged vinegar that can be found in gourmet specialty stores. *Serves 6–8.*

CELERIAC SALAD WITH APPLES & PECANS

1 celery root (celeriac)	With paring knife, cut away coarse outer layer of root. Cut chunks suitable for grating. Using large grater or food processor, grate 3 cups.
1 tart apple	Peel, core and grate. Add to celeriac.

Mustard Mayonnaise:

2 egg yolks 1 1/2 Tbsp. Dijon mustard 1/4 tsp. salt White pepper to taste	Beat together all ingredients.
1 cup light vegetable oil (or peanut oil for extra flavour)	Gradually add the oil, drop by drop at first, then continue beating in very gradually until mixture is thick and creamy.
2–3 Tbsp. lemon juice	Add to dressing to taste. Pour over celeriac and apples.
1/2 cup coarsely chopped toasted pecans	Just before serving, fold in pecans.

Serve on a bed of radicchio or red lettuce. *Serves 4–6.*

SPINACH SALAD WITH PEANUTS, APPLES & MANGO CHUTNEY DRESSING

1 bunch spinach, washed carefully and dried 1 tart green apple, chopped coarsely 1/4 cup chopped green onion 1 cup roasted whole peanuts	Toss together.

Dressing:

1/4 cup lemon juice 2 Tbsp. red wine vinegar 4 Tbsp. mango chutney 1 tsp. curry powder 1/8 tsp. cayenne 1/4 tsp. turmeric 1/2 tsp. sugar 1/2 tsp. salt	Combine in blender and blend for 2 minutes.
3/4 cup light vegetable oil	Gradually add oil, blending until mixture is smooth.
	Toss spinach with dressing and serve immediately.

This is a great recipe! The tangy curry and chutney dressing coats the spinach leaves with a glossy shine. *Serves 4.*

NEW WAVE CAESAR WITH SPINACH & ROMAINE

Preheat oven to 350°F.

Garlic Croutons:

3 Tbsp. butter
3 Tbsp. oil
2 cloves garlic, crushed
1 Tbsp. chopped fresh parsley
8 slices French bread, cubed
(or any leftover good bread, even bagels)

Melt butter, then add oil, garlic and parsley. Toss bread in mixture, coating thoroughly. Place on cookie sheet and bake 15 minutes until crisp.

1 head romaine
1 bunch fresh spinach

Wash, dry and tear greens into bite-sized pieces.

Dressing:

2/3 cup olive oil
1/4 cup lemon juice
1 egg, coddled in boiling water
for 10 seconds
1/2 tsp. salt
1/2 tsp. pepper
1 clove garlic, crushed
1–2 tsp. anchovy paste

Combine in blender and blend well.

Pour dressing over greens. Toss with croutons.

1/2 cup freshly grated Parmesan cheese   Add to salad.

New wave, because it's made with spinach *and* romaine. *Serves 8.*

PASTA PESTO WITH TOASTED WALNUTS

4 cups cooked pasta shells
1 cup chopped fresh parsley
1/2 cup chopped green onion
1 cup coarsely chopped toasted walnuts
1/2 cup Pesto Vinaigrette (*see below*)

Mix well and serve on a bed of lettuce.

Perfect for a summer's picnic! *Serves 4.*

PASTA PRIMAVERA

4 cups cooked rotini or fusilli
1/2 cup chopped red pepper
1/4 cup chopped celery
1/2 cup chopped broccoli
1/2 cup chopped cauliflower
3/4 cup whole snow peas
1/4 cup finely chopped red onion
1/4 cup finely chopped green onion
1/3 cup pine nuts

In a large bowl, mix together.

Pesto Vinaigrette:

1/3 cup fresh lemon juice
1 clove garlic, crushed
Freshly ground pepper

Combine.

2/3 cup olive oil

Gradually beat in oil until dressing has thickened.

3 Tbsp. pesto (*see p. 17*)

Add pesto, beating until smooth.

Pour over pasta and vegetables and toss.

Feel free to mix and match vegetables of the season. *Serves 4.*

MOZZARELLA WITH TOMATOES & BASIL

2 lbs. fresh whole-milk Mozzarella 3 large tomatoes	Slice cheese and tomatoes into 1/2" rounds. Arrange alternately on large platter.
3 Tbsp. chopped fresh basil 1/4 cup balsamic vinegar	Sprinkle with basil and vinegar.
1/3 cup extra virgin olive oil (more, if you prefer)	Pour oil over all.

Balducci's in New York serves this with sundried tomatoes instead of fresh tomatoes. You may want to arrange the cheese and tomatoes on a platter and let your guests choose their own proportions of oil and vinegar. *Serves 6.*

COLD SPAGHETTINI WITH SHRIMP, DILL, SNOW PEAS & RED PEPPERS

6 cups cooked spaghettini or linguine

1 lb. fresh shrimp, shelled, deveined and cooked

2 cups snow peas	Blanch in boiling water 1 minute, then refresh with cold water until chilled.
1 cup thinly sliced red pepper 1/2 cup chopped green onion 1/4 cup chopped fresh parsley 2 Tbsp. chopped fresh dill or 2 tsp. dried dill	Combine in large bowl with cooked shrimp, peas and pasta.

Dressing:

2 cloves garlic, crushed 6 Tbsp. fresh lemon juice Salt and freshly ground white pepper to taste 1 cup light salad oil	Combine, adding the oil last.
	Add to salad and toss. Serve at once.

Serve as a salad course or a main course on a hot summer's day. *Serves 6.*

ASPARAGUS WITH RASPBERRY MOUSSELINE

1 1/2 lbs. fresh asparagus	Steam until just tender and still bright green. (The thinner the stalks, the less cooking time required.)

Mousseline:

1 1/4 cups fresh raspberries or 10 oz. frozen berries, thawed	Puree in food processor or blender. Press through a sieve to remove seeds. Return to processor (or blender).
2 Tbsp. raspberry vinegar 2 Tbsp. lemon juice	Gradually blend in vinegar and lemon juice.
1/2 cup virgin olive oil Pinch of nutmeg Pinch of salt Freshly ground pepper to taste	Slowly add oil and spices, blending until smooth.
1/2 cup heavy cream, whipped until soft and just thickened	Fold gently into dressing. Pour over asparagus. Serve immediately.

Can also be served cold. As soon as asparagus is tender, place stalks under very cold running water until they are chilled. Raspberry vinegar can be found in gourmet specialty stores. *Serves 6–8.*

GREEN BEANS WITH MUSTARD VINAIGRETTE

2 1/2 lbs. green beans	Steam or boil until just tender and still bright green. Refresh under cold running water until cold. Chill.

Mustard Vinaigrette:

1/3 cup white wine vinegar 3–4 Tbsp. Dijon mustard 2 Tbsp. lemon juice	Whisk together.
1/2 cup olive oil 1/2 cup light vegetable oil Salt and freshly ground pepper to taste	Gradually add oils and seasoning, whisking until blended.
	Pour over beans and let marinate for 1 hour before serving.
1/4 cup chopped fresh parsley	Add just before serving.

Serves 6–8.

FRENCH GREEN BEANS WITH RASPBERRY VINAIGRETTE

1 lb. tiny French green beans	Blanch beans in boiling water 3 minutes. Remove from heat and drain, then refresh under cold running water.
1 cup fresh or frozen and thawed raspberries	Place beans and raspberries on a platter.

Raspberry Vinaigrette:

4 Tbsp. raspberry vinegar 1 Tbsp. Dijon mustard }	Whisk together.
10 Tbsp. walnut oil	Gradually add oil until thickened.
Freshly ground pepper to taste	Season with pepper.
	Toss over beans and raspberries. Garnish with additional berries.

Raspberry Vinaigrette makes a beautiful salad dressing over butter lettuce. *Serves 6.*

HEARTS OF PALM & ARTICHOKE HEARTS WITH RASPBERRY VINAIGRETTE

14-oz. tin hearts of palm	Drain, rinse, cut into small pieces and place in a bowl.
14-oz. tin artichoke hearts	Drain, rinse, cut in half and add to above.
Raspberry Vinaigrette (*see above*)	Pour over hearts of palm and artichoke hearts and marinate 3–4 hours before serving.

This salad can marinate overnight for more flavour. *Serves 6–8.*

Quiche & Pizza

TRADITIONAL QUICHE LORRAINE

9" or 10" pie crust, prebaked 5 minutes at 375°F

Preheat oven to 450°F.

6 strips bacon

Cook until crisp. Drain on paper towels. Remove excess fat from skillet.

1 Tbsp. butter
1 large onion, sliced in thin rounds

Sauté onion in butter until transparent.

1/2 cup grated Gruyère cheese
3/4 cup grated Emmenthaler cheese
1/4 cup grated Parmesan cheese

Mix cheeses with crumbled bacon and onion and sprinkle over crust.

3 eggs
1 1/2 cups heavy cream
1/4 tsp. nutmeg
1/2 tsp. salt
1/4 tsp. white pepper

Whisk to blend and pour over cheese mixture.

Bake 10 minutes then reduce heat to 350°F and continue baking for 20–30 minutes. Serve hot.

The first quiche I had in Vancouver was a traditional Quiche Lorraine. We've now introduced lots of new varieties. Read on . . . . *Serves 6–8.*

FRESH SALMON QUICHE

9″ or 10″ pie crust, prebaked 5 minutes at 375°F	Preheat oven to 350°F.
1/2 lb. fresh salmon fillets 1/4 cup white wine 3 slices onion 3 peppercorns 1/4 cup water	Place salmon in skillet or saucepan. Add remaining ingredients and simmer 8–10 minutes until salmon is just firm. Remove salmon with slotted spoon and set aside. (Liquid can be saved for a soup base.)
2 eggs 1 cup light cream 1/4 cup heavy cream Salt and white pepper 3 Tbsp. cream cheese (*optional*)	Blend together well.
1 1/2 cups grated Jarlsberg cheese	Sprinkle cheese on pie crust. Separate salmon gently with hands and layer on cheese.
2 Tbsp. capers	Sprinkle capers over salmon and pour cream mixture over all. Bake 30–35 minutes until firm.

A great way to enjoy our fresh B.C. salmon. Spring or sockeye are my favourites for this. *Serves 6–8.*

FOUR-CHEESE QUICHE WITH RED PEPPER

9″ or 10″ pie crust, prebaked 5 minutes at 375°F	Preheat oven to 400°F.
4 oz. Roquefort or blue cheese, crumbled 3 oz. Swiss cheese, grated 4 oz. Brie, broken into small bits	Mix together.
1 1/2 cups heavy cream 3 eggs 1/8 tsp. nutmeg Salt and pepper 1/4 cup cream cheese	In blender or food processor, blend well together.
1 large or 2 small red bell peppers 2 Tbsp. butter, melted	Slice peppers into rounds, remove seeds and membrane and sauté in butter until soft.
	Sprinkle cheese on crust. Top with sautéed pepper rings. Pour custard over peppers. Bake 10 minutes. Reduce heat to 350°F and continue cooking 20–25 minutes until knife comes out clean.

Rich and creamy with inviting colour. *Serves 6–8.*

FRESH CRAB & SPINACH QUICHE

9″ or 10″ pie shell, prebaked 5 minutes at 375°F	Preheat oven to 350°F.
1 bunch spinach	Wash, stem and steam spinach until wilted. Squeeze out excess water and chop fine.
1/2 lb. fresh Dungeness crab	Add to spinach and mix together.
3 Tbsp. chopped shallots 1 Tbsp. butter	Sauté shallots in butter. Toss with crab/spinach mixture.
2 eggs 1 cup heavy cream 1/4 cup cream cheese 1/4 tsp. salt 1/4 tsp. white pepper Pinch of nutmeg	Mix well with whisk or in blender.
1 cup grated Emmenthaler cheese 1 cup grated Gruyère cheese	Sprinkle a layer of cheese on crust. Toss rest of cheese with spinach/crab mixture and spread on crust.
	Pour cream over all, spreading evenly with your fingers.
	Bake 35–40 minutes until firm (knife comes out clean).

Our West Coast Dungeness crab is a treasured delicacy! *Serves 6–8.*

LAZY GOURMET DEEP-DISH SPINACH & FETA PIE

10″ deep-dish pie crust, prebaked 5 minutes at 375°F	Preheat oven to 350°F.
1 bunch spinach	Wash, stem and steam spinach until wilted. Squeeze out excess water and chop.
3 Tbsp. oil 1 onion, chopped	Heat oil and sauté onion until golden. Toss with spinach.
1 cup grated Swiss cheese	Mix with onion and spinach.
2 eggs 1 1/4 cups light cream 1/2 tsp. salt 1/4 tsp. pepper 1/8 tsp. nutmeg 1/4 cup soft cream cheese	Mix well with whisk or in blender.
	Spread onion/spinach/cheese mixture on crust.
6 oz. Feta cheese, grated or crumbled 2 medium tomatoes, sliced	Top with Feta cheese and decorate with tomatoes.
	Pour on custard, making sure it soaks through to crust. (Use fingers or spoon to spread.) Bake 40–45 minutes.

At The Lazy Gourmet, the Greek influence has hit the quiche. Great hot or at room temperature. *Serves 8.*

NO-FAIL PASTRY

2 1/2 cups all-purpose flour
1/2 tsp. salt
1/2 cup butter
1/2 cup shortening

Cut butter and shortening into flour.

1 egg yolk
Juice of 1/2 lemon
Water

Combine egg yolk and lemon juice and add water to make 1/2 cup of liquid. Add to flour mixture. Mix until just blended. Roll into a ball and refrigerate until ready to use.

Roll out to fit pie plate or flan pan.

Still and always a favourite! *Makes double crust for 9" or 10" pie.*

CREAM CHEESE PASTRY

1 cup butter
6 oz. cream cheese
2 cups all-purpose flour
1/8 tsp. salt

Mix together with pastry blender until thoroughly blended.

Roll out to fit 10" pie plate or flan pan.

For quiches, prebake 7–8 minutes at 375°F.

Also great for tart shells! *Makes 1 crust.*

PIZZA CRUST

1 1/3 cups warm water
1 pkg. dry yeast
1 Tbsp. sugar

Dilute sugar in warm water. Add yeast and let sit 10 minutes.

3 cups flour
2 Tbsp. oil
1 tsp. salt }

Stir into yeast mixture to form dough. Knead until smooth and elastic.

Place dough in oiled bowl and turn to coat all surfaces. Cover with oiled wax paper and let sit in warm place until doubled (about 1 hour). Punch down and stretch to fit 14″ pizza pan or cookie sheet.

Top with any of your favourite toppings and bake 20 minutes at 400°F.

WHOLE WHEAT PIZZA CRUST

1 1/4 cups warm water
1 tsp. sugar
1 pkg. dry yeast

Dilute sugar in warm water. Add yeast and let sit about 5 minutes until foamy.

1 1/4 cups white flour
1 1/4 cups whole wheat flour
1 tsp. salt }

Mix together.

5 Tbsp. vegetable oil

Combine oil, yeast mixture and flours. Knead until smooth and elastic. (If dough sticks to bowl, add a bit more flour; if too dry, add some water, 1 tsp. at a time.)

Transfer to oiled bowl and turn to coat all sides. Cover and let rise in a warm spot until doubled in volume (about 1 hour).

Punch down and proceed with recipe.

After the dough has risen, you can refrigerate it up to three days, or freeze up to three months. To thaw, transfer from freezer to refrigerator for 7–8 hours.

MAKE-YOUR-OWN TOMATO PASTE

2 Tbsp. butter 3 Tbsp. minced shallots	Melt butter in saucepan. Add shallots and stir until translucent.
3 1/2 lbs. tomatoes	Puree in blender or food processor.
	Add tomatoes to shallots in saucepan and bring to a boil. Reduce heat to medium and cook until liquid evaporates and puree is reduced to a thick paste. To prevent burning, stir paste frequently and reduce heat as it gets thicker.
Salt and freshly ground pepper	Season to taste. For an even smoother texture, press through a sieve.

TOMATO SAUCE

2 Tbsp. extra virgin olive oil	Heat oil in saucepan.
2 1/2 lbs. fresh tomatoes	Chop tomatoes and add to oil.
1/4 cup tomato paste 1/2 tsp. dried red pepper flakes 1/2 tsp. sugar 1/2 small carrot, grated 2 Tbsp. minced fresh basil or 1 1/2 tsp. dried basil 1/2 tsp. dried thyme 1/2 tsp. dried oregano 1 clove garlic, crushed Salt and pepper to taste	Add remaining ingredients and cook, stirring occasionally, for 45 minutes to 1 hour.

Italian plum tomatoes are best.

PIZZA WITH SUNDRIED TOMATOES, BELL PEPPERS, WILD MUSHROOMS & CHÈVRE

Dough for 12" pizza (*see p. 37*)	Preheat oven to 475°F.
3–4 Tbsp. butter 2 Tbsp. oil	Heat butter and oil together.
1/4 lb. wild mushrooms, preferably chanterelles 2 cloves garlic, crushed 2 Tbsp. minced shallots	Sauté at least 10 minutes until soft.
2 bell peppers, red or yellow, sliced thin	Add to mushrooms and sauté 4–5 minutes longer.
1/4 cup sundried tomatoes, sliced very thin	Add to above. Sauté 3–4 minutes and set aside.
3 oz. Chèvre (goat cheese) 3 oz. Mozzarella cheese 2 oz. Parmesan cheese	Grate cheeses and set aside.

To Assemble:

1 Tbsp. oil	Brush crust with oil. Spread mushroom/pepper mixture on crust. Sprinkle with tomatoes. Top with cheeses.
	Bake 18–20 minutes.

This pizza is the trendiest you'll find anywhere. Sundried tomatoes can be purchased in Italian specialty stores or gourmet delis. *Serves 6–8.*

FOUR-CHEESE PIZZA

Dough for 12" pizza (*see p. 37*)	Preheat oven to 475°F.
2 oz. Mozzarella cheese 2 oz. Camembert cheese 2 oz. Parmesan cheese 2 oz. Feta cheese	Process cheeses together in food processor (or grate Mozzarella and Parmesan and break soft cheeses into small bits).
1 cup tomato sauce (*see p. 38*)	Spread sauce over crust.
	Cover sauce with cheeses. Bake 18–20 minutes.

The combination of these 4 cheeses has a flavour all its own! *Serves 6–8.*

Photo #4: Pizza with Sundried Tomatoes, Bell Peppers, Wild Mushrooms & Chèvre.

EXTRA-THIN PIZZA WITH SCALLOPS & LEEKS

Pizza dough, 1/2 recipe	Preheat oven to 475°F.
2 Tbsp. oil 12 large fresh scallops	Heat oil in skillet. Sauté scallops quickly.
1 Tbsp. Pernod	Add to skillet and cook 30 seconds longer. Transfer to plate and slice scallops in half.
2 leeks, white part only	Clean thoroughly under running water and cut into thin rounds.
1 1/2 Tbsp. olive oil 1/4 tsp. fennel 1 clove garlic, crushed	Heat oil and seasonings. Sauté leeks until soft (about 10 minutes) stirring occasionally. Set aside.
1/2 cup fresh tomato sauce (*see p. 38*)	Prepare and set aside.
3 oz. Parmesan cheese	Grate and set aside.

To Assemble:

2 tsp. vegetable oil	Oil 14" round pizza pan. Roll dough onto floured surface to about a 9" round. Gently stretch to 12". Brush dough with oil. Spread with tomato sauce. Top with leeks and scallops. Sprinkle with cheese.
	Bake until bottom of crust is golden (about 10 minutes).

Scallops and leeks with Pernod add a delicate touch that definitely makes this a "gourmet pizza." *Serves 6–8.*

EGGPLANT, GARLIC & TOMATO PIZZA

Dough for 12" pizza (*see p. 37*)	Preheat oven to 475°F.
4–6 Tbsp. olive oil 4–6 cloves, garlic sliced very thin	In saucepan, heat oil over medium heat. Sauté garlic until tender, *being careful not to burn*. Remove with slotted spoon.
1 small eggplant, sliced very thin	In same pan, sauté eggplant until very soft and tender.
1/2 cup tomato sauce (*see p. 38*)	Prepare and set aside.
3 tomatoes	Slice and set aside.
3 oz. Parmesan cheese 3–4 oz. Mozzarella cheese	Grate and set aside.

To Assemble:

2 tsp. olive oil	Brush dough with olive oil. Spread sauce over dough. Arrange eggplant, garlic and tomatoes over sauce. Sprinkle with cheeses.
	Bake 18–20 minutes.

This is even better with an extra-thin crust. Make 1/4 or 1/2 pizza dough recipe. Roll out to 9″, then stretch to 12″. Bake only 10 minutes. Japanese eggplants are wonderful if you can find them. *Serves 6–8.*

HOT PEPPER & CHANTERELLES PIZZA

Whole wheat dough for 12″ pizza (*see p. 37*)	Preheat oven to 475°F.
2 small red bell peppers, chopped 2 small jalapeño peppers, chopped 1 hot banana pepper, chopped 1 clove garlic, crushed 3 Tbsp. minced shallots 4–5 Tbsp. oil	Sauté vegetables in oil until very limp, about 7–8 minutes.
3 Tbsp. butter	Add to above.
1/2 lb. chanterelles, well washed and sliced	Add and continue cooking over medium-low heat until mushrooms are very tender, at least 10 minutes.
1/2–3/4 cup tomato sauce (*see p. 38*)	Prepare and set aside.
3–4 oz. Mozzarella cheese 2 oz. Parmesan cheese	Grate and set aside.

To Assemble:

2 tsp. vegetable oil	Oil pizza pan. Roll out dough to 12″. Stretch to edges of pan. Spread sauce over dough. Cover with pepper/mushroom mixture. Top with cheeses.
	Bake 18–20 minutes until bubbly.

Chanterelles are found in B.C. forests every October. At other times of year, use the best mushrooms you can find. They will not take as long to cook. *Serves 6–8.*

Chicken

DIJON CHICKEN IN CREAM SAUCE

Preheat oven to 350°F.

4-lb. roasting chicken,
cut into serving pieces

3 Tbsp. butter
3 Tbsp. oil } Melt in large skillet.

1/2 cup flour
Salt and pepper to taste } Dredge chicken in seasoned flour and brown, skin side down, over medium-high heat 6–7 minutes on each side. Transfer chicken to large baking dish.

1/2 cup Dijon mustard — Coat chicken skin thickly with mustard.

2 Tbsp. butter
1 onion, coarsely chopped
1 clove garlic, crushed — In separate saucepan, sauté onion and garlic.

1 cup mushrooms, sliced — Add to saucepan.

1/3 cup sherry
1/2 cup chicken stock } Add and cook 3–4 minutes until slightly reduced.

1 1/2 cups heavy cream — Remove mixture from heat and add cream, combining well. Return to medium heat and simmer 5–6 minutes until slightly thickened.

Pour over chicken and bake 35–40 minutes until chicken tests done.

People ask me for this recipe all the time. Wild rice is a perfect accompaniment. For 121 recipes for cooking with chicken, see my twin sister Lynn's first cookbook, *Chicken! Chicken! Chicken!* (Whitecap Books, 1985). *Serves 4–6.*

PECAN CRISPY CHICKEN

Preheat oven to 350°F.

8 chicken breasts, boned — Pound between 2 layers of wax paper with mallet or cleaver until flat.

1/2 cup flour
Salt and pepper to taste } Dredge in seasoned flour.

6 Tbsp. Dijon mustard
3/4 cup melted butter
2 Tbsp. lime juice
1 egg, beaten — Whisk mustard. Add butter, lime juice and egg. Whisk until well mixed. Dip breasts in sauce.

1 1/2 cups finely chopped pecans
1 1/2 cups fine bread crumbs } Combine and coat chicken pieces. Cover with wax paper and chill 1–2 hours.

Place chicken on cookie sheet and bake 35–40 minutes.

1 lime, sliced — Serve with a slice of lime on each piece of chicken.

An '80s version of crispy fried chicken. Serve on a bed of wild rice with a steamed vegetable. *Serves 6–8.*

GRANDMA FAYE'S STICKY APRICOT CHICKEN

Preheat oven to 375°F.

4-lb. roasting chicken — Cut chicken into serving pieces.

1 cup apricot jam
1/2 cup chili sauce
1/4 cup dry white wine
2 Tbsp. soy sauce
2 Tbsp. honey
1 tsp. grated fresh ginger
1/4 tsp. salt } Combine and heat, whisking until well blended.

Place chicken in baking pan. Baste thoroughly with sauce. Bake 1 1/2 hours until chicken tests done and surface is sticky.

5 oz. dried apricots — Top with apricots during last 1/2 hour of cooking time.

Your guests will call it gourmet, you'll call it easy! *Serves 4–6.*

LYLA'S CRANBERRY-ORANGE CHICKEN

Preheat oven to 375°F.

4-lb. chicken,
cut into serving pieces

Bake 15 minutes, skin side down. Turn.

14-oz. can whole cranberry sauce
1/4 cup orange juice concentrate
1/4 cup soy sauce
1/3 cup honey

While chicken is baking, combine ingredients in medium saucepan. Bring to a boil, lower heat and let simmer 5 minutes.

Pour sauce over chicken. Bake 1–1 1/2 hours. The longer you bake, the stickier it will get. You can turn the pieces every 1/2 hour to make sure they are well coated.

A Friday night special in our home, now on The Lazy Gourmet hit parade! *Serves 4–6.*

BROILED CHICKEN WITH PEANUT SAUCE

4 whole chicken breasts

Skin, bone and halve.

1/3 cup light vegetable oil
1 Tbsp. fresh lemon juice
1 clove garlic, crushed
1/2 tsp. cumin
1/2 tsp. thyme
1/4 tsp. salt

Mix together.

Marinate chicken breasts for 5 minutes. Drain and broil on each side 4–5 minutes until cooked through.

Pour marinade over chicken.

1 cup light cream
1/2 cup peanut butter
1/4 cup soy sauce or Tamari
1 Tbsp. lemon juice
2 cloves garlic, crushed
1 1/2 tsp. dry mustard
1 Tbsp. butter

Combine in medium saucepan and blend with a whisk. Bring to a boil, then simmer 3–4 minutes. Pour over chicken.

You'll need two saucepans, but this recipe is worth the extra dishes. Serve with wild rice and steamed snow peas. *Serves 6–8.*

BARBARA LARABIE'S ASIAN CHICKEN

3 1/2-lb. frying chicken, cut into small pieces
3 Tbsp. oil

Heat oil in large skillet. Fry chicken, browning on all sides. Drain off most of fat.

2 whole heads of garlic (*yes!*)

Slice garlic into fine bits and add to chicken. Fry until garlic is soft.

1/4 cup soy sauce
3/4 cup wine vinegar
3–4 Tbsp. honey
2 whole dried peppers, cut into pieces

Combine and add to skillet. Cook until the sauce is thick enough to coat chicken.

1/2 cup roasted whole peanuts (*optional*)

Add to chicken just before serving.

If one person in the crowd eats this chicken, everyone must! For true garlic-lovers only! Serve on a bed of Colourful Rice Pilaf (*see p. 74*) with a steamed vegetable. *Serves 4.*

HONEY GARLIC CHICKEN WINGS

2 doz. chicken wings

Preheat oven to 375°F.

2 cloves garlic, crushed
2 tsp. grated fresh ginger
2 Tbsp. honey
3 Tbsp. brown sugar
1/2 cup soy sauce or Tamari

Mix together. Pour over wings and toss.

Place wings on baking sheet and bake 45 minutes.

1/4 cup honey
1/4 cup sesame seeds, toasted

Drizzle honey over wings and sprinkle with seeds.

Bake an additional 15 minutes.

This can also be served in a chafing dish as a hot hors d'oeuvre. The sauce can be used with any chicken pieces. *Serves 6.*

CHICKEN KIEV WITH SESAME SEEDS

1/2 cup butter
2 Tbsp. Dijon mustard
1 tsp. lemon juice
1–2 Tbsp. chopped fresh parsley

Mix together well, roll into 8 balls and chill thoroughly.

4 whole chicken breasts

Skin, bone and halve. Pound between sheets of wax paper with mallet or cleaver until flat.

Put a butter ball in the centre of each chicken piece and fold the meat around it. Be sure that the butter is completely encased. Chill 1 hour.

Preheat oven to 400°F.

1/2 cup flour
Salt and pepper to taste

Dredge breasts in seasoned flour.

2 eggs, beaten

Dip breasts in eggs.

1 1/4 cups fine bread crumbs
1/4 cup sesame seeds

Combine and cover breasts with crumb mixture.

Vegetable oil for frying

Heat oil in deep pot and fry chicken until browned. Drain on paper towels, then bake on cookie sheet for 20 minutes.

The test for perfect Chicken Kiev: when a knife is first inserted, the butter will spurt into your eyes! Serve with rice pilaf and a vegetable. *Serves 8.*

DELICIOUS SESAME BAKED CHICKEN

5-lb. roasting chicken

Cut chicken into serving pieces.

2–3 large cloves garlic, crushed
4 Tbsp. fresh lemon juice
3/4 cup light vegetable oil

Combine.

Pour marinade over chicken and refrigerate 3–4 hours.

Preheat oven to 375°F.

1 1/4 cups fine bread crumbs
(or corn flake crumbs)
3 Tbsp. finely chopped fresh parsley
6 Tbsp. sesame seeds
1/2 tsp. salt
Pepper to taste

Roll chicken in seasoned crumb mixture. Place on baking sheet and bake for 1 hour until chicken is tender.

Unbelievably simple! Serve cold the next day for another treat. *Serves 4–6.*

CHICKEN WITH CHANTERELLES

Preheat oven to 350°F.

4 chicken breasts, cut in half
3 Tbsp. butter or oil

Heat butter in skillet. Fry chicken on both sides for 3–4 minutes. Place in casserole dish.

3 Tbsp. butter
4 shallots, minced
2 cloves garlic, minced

Sauté shallots and garlic in butter until soft.

1/2 lb. chanterelles, well washed and sliced

Add mushrooms and cook until soft. (Chanterelles take a lot longer to cook than regular mushrooms, so test to make sure they are completely done.)

3 Tbsp. butter
3 Tbsp. flour

In separate pan, melt butter and whisk in flour.

3 cups light cream
1/4 cup heavy cream
3 Tbsp. sherry

Add very gradually to butter/flour mixture.

Add chanterelles and simmer 2–3 minutes.

Cover chicken breasts with sauce and bake 35–40 minutes.

Try to refrain from nibbling the chanterelles — or start with 1 lb. and no one will know!
Serves 4.

Fish & Seafood

HALIBUT WITH SWEET RED PEPPER SAUCE

3–4 red bell peppers, roasted and peeled (*see p. 25*)

Puree in food processor or blender.

2 Tbsp. heavy cream
1/4 tsp. sugar
2 tsp. fresh lemon juice
2 Tbsp. soft unsalted butter

Add to peppers and process until smooth. Place in top of double boiler and keep warm.

2 lbs. halibut fillets or steaks

Poach or fry fish. When it flakes easily, pour sauce over fish.

Serves 4–6.

RED BELL PEPPER SAUCE

2 large red bell peppers, roasted and peeled (*see p. 25*)

Puree in food processor or blender.

1/2 cup dry white wine
1/3 cup white wine vinegar

Boil together until reduced to 1/4 cup.

1 tsp. chopped fresh basil
Salt and pepper to taste

Add seasonings and pureed peppers to liquid.

9 Tbsp. butter

Whisk into sauce 1 Tbsp. at a time until well blended and thickened.

Pour over poached or fried fish.

Red bell pepper sauce is all the rage these days. It's especially good with halibut.

SUSIE & PETER'S HAZELNUT LEMON HALIBUT

Preheat oven to 350°F.

2 lbs. halibut fillets

1 cup fine bread crumbs 1/2 cup coarsely chopped hazelnuts Salt and pepper to taste Grated rind of 1 lemon 2–3 Tbsp. chopped fresh parsley	Mix together and set aside.
Juice of 1 lemon	Squeeze over halibut.
1/2 cup flour Salt and pepper	Dredge fish in seasoned flour.
1 egg 2 Tbsp. cream	Beat together. Dip fish in egg mixture.
	Now dip in hazelnut mixture.
4–6 Tbsp. butter or oil, or a combination	Fry halibut on each side, 3–4 minutes depending on thickness of fish, until light brown and crisp.
Lemon slices Fresh parsley	Transfer fish to baking sheet. Bake 8–10 minutes. Garnish with lemon slices and parsley sprigs and serve immediately.

This is one of my favourite recipes! It is also excellent with snapper, cod or any white fish. *Serves 4–6.*

FRESH HALIBUT WITH BASIL & PARSLEY SAUCE

1/2 cup white wine 1/4 cup lemon juice	Combine in medium saucepan and cook 2–3 minutes.
1 cup heavy cream	Add to above and cook until liquid is reduced by half (to 3/4 cup).
1/4 cup chopped fresh parsley 1/4 cup finely chopped fresh basil 1 Tbsp. capers Salt and pepper to taste	Add and whisk until well blended. Set aside.
2 lbs. halibut fillets	
1/2 cup flour Salt and freshly ground pepper	Dredge fish lightly in seasoned flour.

(Cont'd over)

1/2 cup butter

In large skillet, heat butter, add fish and fry on high heat until fish just starts to flake. The trick is not to overcook it. Keep testing.

Reheat sauce, pour over fish and serve at once.

For this recipe, fillets are preferable to steaks. If fresh halibut is in season, treat yourself to a thick centre cut. *Serves 4–6.*

POACHED HALIBUT WITH SHRIMP & SUNDRIED TOMATOES

Preheat oven to 400°F.

2 lbs. halibut fillets or steaks
1/4 cup fresh lemon juice
3 Tbsp. butter

Place fish in large buttered casserole. Sprinkle with lemon juice and dot with butter.

Cover with foil, sealing well. Bake 15 minutes.

4 Tbsp. butter
2 Tbsp. shallots, minced
1 clove garlic, crushed

Sauté shallots and garlic in butter until transparent.

6 oz. fresh shrimp, shelled and deveined

Add shrimp and cook until pink and firm (about 3 minutes).

3 oz. sundried tomatoes, sliced thin

Add to shrimp and cook 3–4 minutes.

5 oz. snow peas

Steam 2 minutes.

Remove fish from oven. Cover with shrimp and tomatoes. Top with snow peas (or serve peas on the side).

As sundried tomatoes are very salty, you'll find no salt in this recipe! *Serves 6.*

PAN-FRIED SNAPPER WITH PECAN BUTTER SAUCE

4 – 6 oz. red snapper fillets	Rinse and set aside.

Pecan Butter Sauce:

5 Tbsp. butter 1/2 cup chopped pecans 2 Tbsp. chopped red onion 1 clove garlic, crushed 1 Tbsp. lemon juice 3–4 dashes hot pepper sauce	Combine in food processor or blender until smooth.

Seafood Sauce:

4 Tbsp. butter 2 Tbsp. flour	Melt butter and add flour, stirring until well blended.
1 clove garlic, crushed 1 cup fish stock (*see p. 65*) 1/4 cup white wine	Add slowly to butter/flour mixture and cook until thickened, stirring constantly. Keep warm.

4 – 6 oz. red snapper fillets

1 egg 4 Tbsp. cream 3 Tbsp. milk	Whisk together in shallow dish.
1 cup flour 1/2 tsp. pepper 1/2 tsp. salt 1/4 tsp. dry mustard 1/8 tsp. cayenne	Combine in separate dish.
	Dredge snapper fillets in seasoned flour. Dip in egg/cream mixture. Wipe off excess liquid with paper towel. Dredge again in flour.
Light vegetable oil for frying	Fry fillets in hot oil until golden, 3–4 minutes on each side.
8 Tbsp. whole pecans	To serve: place some seafood sauce on individual dish. Top with fish fillet. Top with warmed pecan sauce. Sprinkle with whole pecans.

This is a very rich main course, so serve with a light salad. *Serves 4.*

FRESH RED SNAPPER WITH EGGPLANT & CURRY

1 1/2 lbs. red snapper fillets	Rinse and set aside.
Curry Sauce:	
1 Tbsp. butter 2 shallots, minced	Sauté shallots in butter until soft.
1 Tbsp. grated fresh ginger 3 cloves garlic, crushed	Add and stir 1 minute.
2 tsp. curry powder 1/8 tsp. cayenne 1/4 tsp. turmeric	Add and stir 1 minute.
1 cup fish stock (*see p. 65*)	Add and bring to boil on medium heat. Continue to cook until liquid is reduced to 1/3 cup.
1 1/2 cups heavy cream	Add and bring to a slow boil. Simmer until sauce is thickened.
Salt and pepper to taste	Season sauce and set aside.
1/2 lb. Japanese eggplant Salt	Slice into 1/2″ slices. Sprinkle with salt.
3 Tbsp. butter 1 Tbsp. olive oil	Sauté eggplant in oil/butter mixture until brown. Cover and cook until very soft (another 5–7 minutes). Do not undercook.
3 Tbsp. butter	Heat butter in skillet and fry snapper fillets on each side until just starting to flake.
	To serve: cover with eggplant and smother with sauce.

This sauce is also delicious with our local cod or halibut. *Serves 4.*

SALMON FLORENTINE IN PHYLLO

Preheat oven to 400°F.

6 – 6-oz.-thick fillets of sockeye or spring salmon
Juice of 1 lemon

Sprinkle lemon over salmon. Set aside.

1 large bunch spinach

Steam until just wilted. Squeeze out excess water.

1 small onion, chopped very fine
1 clove garlic, minced
2 Tbsp. butter

Sauté onion and garlic in butter until soft.

Salt and pepper
Dash of nutmeg

In food processor or blender, combine spinach, onion/garlic mixture and seasonings until very smooth.

Remove skin from fillets. Cut a pocket in each fillet and fill with spinach mixture.

1 lb. phyllo (30 sheets)
1/2 cup butter, melted

Place 5 large sheets of phyllo, one on top of the other, in baking pan, brushing each layer with butter.

Place 1 salmon fillet at bottom centre of sheets. Fold sides of pastry towards centre, then fold from bottom up to enclose and seal fish. Repeat for each fillet.

Brush top of each packet with melted butter. Bake 22–25 minutes until flaky and brown.

Truly a West Coast delicacy! *Serves 6.*

SPECTACULAR DECORATED BAKED SALMON

I.

Preheat oven to 375°F.

6-lb. spring or sockeye salmon, stuffed (*see following pages for stuffings*).

Fish should be butterflied (head and tail on, but centre bone removed).

Make wrapper for fish by folding edges of 2 large pieces of foil together.

Place stuffed salmon on foil so that back is up and stuffed portion is down.

1/2 cup white wine
Juice of 1 lemon
Light sprinkling of salt and pepper

Combine and brush over back of fish.

Wrap foil loosely around fish, leaving room inside for steam to circulate. Bake 1 hour and 20 minutes.

To check for doneness, open foil at top and insert small knife in flesh. If it flakes, it is ready. If not, cover and return to oven for 5–10 more minutes. *Try not to overcook!*

Serve with blender hollandaise (*see p. 60*).

Serves 12.

II.

6-lb. salmon, prepared as above

Remove skin while fish is still warm (it will peel off). Cool to room temperature. Wrap in plastic wrap and chill 4–5 hours or overnight.

Place salmon on large platter on bed of lettuce or spinach leaves.

1 large English cucumber
2 large lemons

Slice as thinly as possible. Cover the fish as completely as possible with the cucumber slices to give the appearance of scales. Place lemon slices at random or down the centre of the fish.

Serve with lime mayonnaise (*see p. 61*) or cucumber-dill sauce (*see p. 61*).

Serves 12.

Photo #5: Raspberry-Blueberry Cornmeal Muffins (*at top*), Canadian Wild Rice (*in basket*) and Cold Poached Decorated Salmon (*in foreground*).

WILD RICE STUFFING FOR SALMON

2 cups cooked wild rice	Put 3/4 cup rice in 2 1/2 cups boiling water. Lower heat and simmer 30–40 minutes.
3 Tbsp. butter 1 large onion, chopped 3–4 stalks celery, chopped 1/2 red bell pepper, chopped 1/2 lb. mushrooms, sliced	Melt butter in saucepan. Sauté vegetables in the order given until tender.
1 1/2 cups croutons	Add to cooked vegetables. Add cooked rice.
1/2 cup pecans, toasted 3 Tbsp. sherry 3 Tbsp. soy sauce 1 Tbsp. chopped fresh thyme or 1 tsp. dried thyme 1 Tbsp. chopped fresh basil or 1 tsp dried basil Salt and freshly ground pepper to taste	Mix together and add to above.
	Fill cavity of salmon with mixture and bake as directed.

Chewy, nutty — sensational!

OYSTER STUFFING FOR SALMON

2 lbs. shucked oysters, thoroughly rinsed	Cut each oyster into 4–6 pieces, depending on size.
3 Tbsp. butter 1 onion, chopped 1 clove garlic, crushed	Melt butter and sauté onion and garlic until soft.
2 Tbsp. Pernod	Add Pernod and oysters and cook 1 minute.
1 large bunch parsley, chopped 1 cup fine bread crumbs	Add to above and mix.
Salt and pepper	Season to taste.
	Fill cavity of salmon with mixture and bake as directed.

For a delicious variation, substitute spinach for parsley. Use 1 bunch of spinach, steam until wilted, squeeze out excess water, chop and add to recipe.

Photo #6: Fresh Halibut with Basil & Parsley Sauce (*at top*) and Asparagus with Raspberry Mousseline (*lower left*).

SEAFOOD STUFFING FOR SALMON

6 Tbsp. butter 2 medium onions, minced 1 1/2 cups finely chopped mushrooms	Melt butter in medium saucepan, then sauté onions and mushrooms until soft.
3 cloves garlic, crushed	Add and sauté until tender but not browned.
2 medium bunches parsley	Chop well and stir into above. Remove from heat.
1/2 cup fine bread crumbs	Add to above.
4 oz. crabmeat 4 oz. shrimp, shelled and deveined 4 oz. scallops 2 tsp. lemon juice	Cut in small pieces, toss together and add.
1/4 tsp. cayenne Salt and pepper to taste	Add and combine well.
	Fill cavity of salmon with mixture and bake as directed.

Expensive to make, but well worth it!

FABULOUS BLENDER HOLLANDAISE

3 egg yolks 2 Tbsp. fresh lemon juice 1/4 tsp. salt 1/4 tsp. ground white pepper	Combine well in blender.
1/2 cup butter	In a small saucepan, heat butter until foamy. Skim off the white solids.
	Turn on blender to highest speed. Pour the hot butter into egg yolk mixture, at first in droplets, then in a *slow*, steady stream until it is a thick cream.

Amazingly easy to make!

CUCUMBER-DILL SAUCE

1/4 English cucumber	Chop very fine.
1/4 tsp. salt	Toss cucumber with salt. Let sit for 15 minutes.
1/2 cup plain yogurt 1 cup sour cream 1 tsp. lemon juice White pepper to taste 3 green onions, finely chopped (white part only) 2 tsp. chopped fresh dill or 1 tsp. dried dill	Combine thoroughly.
	Squeeze water from cucumber and add to above.

A lower calorie accompaniment to any fresh fish dish if you reverse the proportions and use 1 cup plain yogurt to 1/2 cup sour cream.

LIME MAYONNAISE

2 large egg yolks 2 tsp. Dijon mustard 1 tsp. lime juice Ground white pepper	Combine in a food processor or blender or beat well with a whisk.
1/2 cup peanut or olive oil	Add to above, 1 drop at a time, until thickened.
1 cup peanut oil	Add to above in a *slow*, steady stream.
1–2 Tbsp. lime juice 1/4 tsp. salt Ground white pepper	Combine and add.
Rind of 1 lime, finely grated	Add to above.

Serve in a small bowl. Decorate with a lime slice. A perfect accompaniment to cold poached salmon!

BARBECUED SALMON TERIYAKI

3 lbs. salmon fillets, skin on

1 cup soy sauce or Tamari 1/4 cup sherry 4 Tbsp. honey 2 cloves garlic, crushed 2 Tbsp. grated fresh ginger	Combine. Marinate fish for 1 hour.

Vegetable oil	Brush flesh side of fillets with oil. Place on hot barbecue and grill for 30 seconds. Turn to skin side and grill until fish just starts to flake. Additional marinade may be brushed on while grilling.
	Serve with mustard sauce (*see below or p. 63*)

Serves 6–8.

COOKED MUSTARD SAUCE

3 eggs 1 cup heavy cream 1/4 cup butter 1 Tbsp. red wine vinegar 6 Tbsp. Dijon mustard	Combine in top of double boiler and cook over simmering water, whisking until thickened.
	Serve warm.

This tangy sauce can be served with any grilled fish.

HONEY MUSTARD SAUCE

1 – 6 oz. jar Dijon mustard
1 1/2 cups mayonnaise
2 Tbsp. honey
2 Tbsp. freshly squeezed lemon juice

} Whisk together.

BUTTER LEMON GARLIC BASTE
(FOR BARBECUED SALMON)

1/2 cup butter

In a small saucepan, heat butter until foamy. Clarify (skim off the white solids).

Juice of 1 1/2 lemons
1–2 cloves garlic, crushed
2 Tbsp. chopped fresh parsley

} Whisk together thoroughly and combine with butter.

Brush on salmon for barbecuing or grilling.

Makes enough for 2 lbs. of fish.

WEST COAST PAELLA

1 1/2 lbs. large shrimp 1/2 lb. fresh scallops 2 doz. clams 2 doz. mussels	Shell and devein shrimp. Wash mussels and clams well. Set aside.
1 1/2 lbs. chicken	Cut into small serving pieces.
1 tsp. oregano 1 clove garlic, crushed Salt and coarsely ground pepper to taste 2 Tbsp. olive oil 1 tsp. wine vinegar	Combine well and rub into chicken.
4 Tbsp. oil	In large, deep skillet, preferably a paella pan, heat oil and brown chicken.
2 oz. ham, sliced thin 2 oz. hot sausage, preferably Spanish, sliced 1 large onion, chopped 1 red bell pepper, chopped 1/2 tsp. ground coriander	Add to chicken and cook 10 minutes.
1/4 cup tomato sauce 2 1/2 cups long grain rice	Stir into above and cook 4–5 minutes.
4 cups water 1 tsp. saffron *(threads only!)*	In saucepan, bring water and saffron to a boil.
	Add water and shrimp to chicken and cook, covered, until liquid is absorbed (about 20 minutes).
1 1/4 cups fresh or frozen, thawed peas	Add peas and scallops and cook 5 minutes longer.
	Steam mussels and clams in a small amount of water just until the shells start to open.
	Add to above and serve hot.

A West Coast seafood bounty! *Serves 10.*

SEVICHE

1 1/2 lbs. fresh scallops
1 cup fresh lime juice

Place scallops in glass bowl. Add lime juice and toss. Cover and let sit 4 hours.

1 medium onion, thinly sliced
1 large tomato, peeled and diced
1/4 cup finely chopped fresh parsley
1/4 cup extra virgin olive oil
3 small jalapeño peppers, finely chopped
Salt to taste

Combine and add to scallops. Cover and let sit 4 more hours.

Lettuce
Lime slices

Arrange on a bed of lettuce and garnish with lime slices.

This makes a refreshing first course. *Serves 6–8.*

VERY SIMPLE FISH STOCK

1 1/2 lbs. fish pieces:
bones, tails, heads, etc.

Rinse well. Place in pot.

1 Tbsp. butter
1 onion, sliced

In separate pan, sauté onion in butter, then add to stock pot.

4–5 parsley stems
2 bay leaves
Pinch of thyme
1 small carrot
Water

Add, cover with water and bring to a boil. Simmer for 1/2 hour. Skim surface and strain through a sieve.

Make extra quantities and freeze. Great for poaching fish or as a base for fish stews and chowders.

Veal & Beef

BEEF STROGANOFF

2 lbs. sirloin, sliced 1/4" thick 1/2 cup butter	Brown strips of meat well in butter. Remove from pan, but keep warm.
2 cups coarsely chopped onion 2 cloves garlic, minced	Add to pan and cook until tender.
1/2 lb. mushrooms, sliced	Add and cook until tender.
2 Tbsp. flour Salt and pepper 12 oz. bouillon or beef stock	Stir flour into vegetables. Season to taste. Add bouillon and cook, stirring constantly, until thickened.
1/4 cup dry white wine 1 cup sour cream 1 tsp. Worcestershire sauce Handful of chopped fresh parsley	Combine and add.
1 lb. dry fettuccine or 1 1/2 lbs. fresh 2–3 Tbsp. butter	Cook fettuccine in boiling, salted water 8–10 minutes for dry; 5–6 minutes for fresh. Drain and toss with butter.
	Return meat to pan and cook until reheated.
Fresh parsley, chopped	Serve meat on a bed of noodles. Sprinkle with parsley before serving.

This old-time favourite has always been popular! Best made at the last minute. Serve with a steamed green vegetable. *Serves 6–8.*

BEEF BOURGIGNON

	Preheat oven to 350° F.
5 lbs. chuck beef	Cut into cubes.
1/2 cup flour Salt and pepper }	Roll beef cubes in seasoned flour.
1/4 cup butter 1/4 cup oil }	Heat in skillet, then brown beef.
2 oz. brandy	Add to skillet and ignite. When flame dies down, transfer meat and juices to large casserole.
1/2 lb. bacon 4 cloves garlic 2 leeks, washed 2 carrots 3 onions 2 Tbsp. fresh parsley }	Chop all coarsely and add to skillet. Cook until bacon is crisp and vegetables are browned. Add to casserole.
2 bay leaves 1 tsp. dried thyme 3 cups Burgundy wine }	Add seasonings and wine to casserole.
Water	Add water to just cover meat. Cook 1 1/2 hours.
1 Tbsp. butter 1 Tbsp. flour }	Make a roux by mixing butter and flour. Add bit by bit to casserole and cook 2–3 hours longer.
3 large onions, cut into large chunks Sprinkling of sugar 2–3 Tbsp. butter }	Sprinkle sugar over onions and sauté in butter until golden brown.
1/4 cup red wine	Add to onions and cook, covered, for 15 minutes.
1 lb. mushroom caps 2 Tbsp. butter }	Brown mushrooms in butter until just tender, turning to cook both sides.
Juice of 1/2 lemon	Sprinkle over mushrooms.
Fresh parsley, chopped	To serve, add onions to casserole, decorate top with mushrooms and sprinkle with parsley.

The Burgundy wine elevates the chuck beef to a gourmet extravagance! A meal in itself! Serve with a light salad. *Serves 10–12.*

BREAST OF VEAL FLORENTINE

	Preheat oven to 325°F.
4 lbs. breast of veal	Cut a deep pocket in side of veal.
3 Tbsp. onion, minced 6 oz. sausage, cut into small pieces 4 Tbsp. butter	Sauté onion and sausage in butter. Drain off fat and place in large mixing bowl.
2–3 bunches spinach	Steam until wilted, then squeeze out excess moisture and chop.
1 cup fine bread crumbs 4 eggs, beaten 1 tsp. salt Pepper to taste	Combine and add to spinach, then add to onion/sausage mixture.
Salt and pepper	Season outside of veal. Stuff pocket with dressing. Skewer ends, or sew up. Place fat side up in roaster and bake for 2 1/2 hours.

Organize yourself by preparing this veal dish ahead of time! Serve with a light salad. *Serves 6–8.*

VEAL SCALOPINE AL MARSALA

2 lbs. veal scallops	Cover with wax paper and pound with wooden mallet or cleaver until 1/8" thin.
1/2 cup flour Salt and pepper	Dredge meat with seasoned flour.
4 Tbsp. butter 4 Tbsp. oil	Combine in skillet. Brown veal on both sides.
3 cups sliced mushrooms	Add to pan and cook 10 minutes, stirring occasionally.
Juice of 1 lemon 3/4 cup Marsala	Add and simmer 5 minutes more.

People love this because it's so easy! Ask your butcher to scallop the veal for you. Serve with fresh boiled potatoes and a steamed vegetable. *Serves 6–8.*

EASY LEMON VEAL

1 1/2 lbs. veal	Ask your butcher to pound until thin; or pound with wooden mallet between two layers of wax paper.
2 eggs, beaten	Dip veal in eggs.
3/4 cup flour Salt and pepper }	Dredge in seasoned flour.
2 Tbsp. oil 2 Tbsp. butter }	Brown veal on both sides in oil/butter mixture. Transfer to warm platter.
2 Tbsp. butter Juice of 1 large lemon }	Add to skillet and whisk vigorously until all browned bits are incorporated. When juice is bubbling, pour over veal.
Lemon slices Fresh parsley	Garnish with lemon slices and parsley.

Serve with asparagus when in season or green beans for a light accent! A lightly roasted potato would also go well with this. *Serves 6.*

TEXAS-STYLE BARBECUE SAUCE FOR RIBS

1/2 cup vinegar 1 Tbsp. Worcestershire sauce 1 large onion, chopped 2 cloves garlic, crushed Juice of 1 large lemon Grated peel of 1 lemon 1/2 cup chili sauce 1/2 tsp. hot pepper sauce 1 tsp. salt 1/2 tsp. chili powder Black pepper to taste }	Combine all ingredients in saucepan. Simmer 15 minutes.
4 lbs. back ribs	Brush ribs with sauce. Barbecue, basting continuously. Save extra sauce to serve on the side.

Make extra as this sauce will keep in your refrigerator for up to 4 weeks. *Serves 6.*

Casseroles, Vegetable Side Dishes & Rice

SEAFOOD PASTA CASSEROLE

9″ × 13″ deep-dish casserole	Preheat oven to 350° F.
1/2 lb. shrimp, shelled and deveined 1/2 lb. scallops (halved if large) 1/4 cup white wine	Toss together and set aside.
1 lb. dry fettuccine or 1 1/2 lbs. fresh fettuccine	Cook in boiling, salted water 8–10 minutes for dry; 5–6 minutes for fresh. Drain and set aside.

Béchamel Sauce:

1/2 cup butter 1/2 cup chopped onion 1 clove garlic, crushed	Melt butter. Sauté onion and garlic until soft.
1/2 cup flour 2 tsp. dry mustard	Add and cook 1 minute, stirring constantly.
2 cups milk 1 1/2 cups light cream	Add gradually, stirring constantly until thickened.
1/2 tsp. ground rosemary 1/4 tsp. cayenne 1 tsp. dried thyme	Add to sauce and stir.
1 1/4 cups grated Swiss cheese 1/4 cup chopped fresh parsley	Stir into sauce.
	Mix together pasta, seafood and sauce. Pour into casserole.
1/2 cup pine nuts 1/4 cup chopped fresh parsley	Sprinkle nuts and parsley over top.
	Bake 30–35 minutes.

For a hungry crowd, this is the West Coast's answer to lasagna! *Serves 6–8.*

CHICKEN AVOCADO CASSEROLE

9″ × 13″ casserole dish	Preheat oven to 350°F.
2 1/2 lbs. chicken breasts, boned 3 Tbsp. oil	Cut chicken into chunks and sauté 5 minutes. Place in casserole.
2 medium-sized avocados	Peel and cut into chunks. Place over chicken.
Béchamel Sauce (*see p. 70*)	Make Béchamel Sauce, pour into casserole and bake 25 minutes.

Don't be afraid to bake the avocados — the flavour and texture is superb! Serve on a bed of Colourful Rice Pilaf (*see p. 74*). *Serves 8.*

CHICKEN PESTO PASTA CASSEROLE

9″ × 13″ deep-dish casserole	Preheat oven to 350°F.
2 lbs. breast of chicken, boned 2–3 Tbsp. butter	Cut chicken into small pieces. Sauté in butter until white and firm.
1 lb. rotini or fusilli (fresh or dry)	Cook in boiling, salted water: 7–8 minutes for fresh; 10–12 minutes for dry.
1/2 cup chopped onion 1/2 cup butter	Sauté onion in butter until transparent.
1/2 cup flour 1 tsp. dried mustard	Add flour and mustard and cook 1 minute, stirring constantly.
2 cups milk 1 1/2 cups light cream 1/2 cup heavy cream	Add very gradually to onion/flour mixture, whisking until thick.
1/3–1/2 cup pesto (*see p. 17*)	Stir in pesto.
	Mix sauce, chicken and pasta together. Place in casserole.
1/4 cup grated Parmesan cheese 1/3 cup pine nuts	Sprinkle cheese and nuts over top. Bake 15 minutes.

This dish can be prepared ahead of time and frozen until ready to cook. *Serves 6–8.*

LAZY GOURMET FETTUCCINE LASAGNA

9″ x 13″ deep-dish casserole, oiled

Preheat oven to 350º F.

3 1/2 cups tomato sauce (*your favourite, or see p. 38*)

1 lb. dry fettuccine or
1 1/2 lbs. fresh fettuccine

Cook in boiling, salted water 8–10 minutes for dry; 5–6 minutes for fresh.

4 oz. Swiss cheese, grated
4 oz. Mozzarella cheese, grated
1/2 cup grated Parmesan cheese

Mix cheeses together, reserving 1 cup for topping.

Custard:

2 eggs
1 1/2 cups Ricotta cheese
Pinch of nutmeg
Salt and pepper to taste

Mix together and set aside.

To Assemble:

Combine noodles, cheese and tomato sauce. Put half the mixture in casserole.

Spoon custard over noodles and spread to cover. Top with remaining noodles and sprinkle with reserved cheese. Bake 30–35 minutes until bubbly.

This recipe was first served to me at Balducci's in New York City six years ago. We've been making it at The Lazy Gourmet daily ever since, and it continues to be a bestseller. *Serves 6–8.*

SIDE VEGETABLES

We on the West Coast have very strong feelings about how our side vegetables should be prepared. Most people I know either steam or wok-fry their vegetables. I have a wonderful bamboo steamer in my home that stacks in compartments, one on top of the other. The heaviest vegetables can be placed in the bottom of the steamer where they are closest to the boiling water, the lightest ones go on top, and they will all be ready at the same time. Stir-fried or wok-fried vegetables are fried very quickly in a little of the lightest safflower or peanut oil. This way, the vegetables are still very tender and bright-coloured when you serve them.

Here is a list of some of our favourite vegetables and the amount of time it takes to steam or stir–fry them. If you steam them, just before serving top with a squeeze of fresh lemon and 1–2 Tbsp. of melted butter and, if available, a sprinkling of fresh herbs.

Fiddlehead Greens grow in our B.C. forests, though they are more commonly found in New Brunswick. Fresh ones should be carefully washed as they have a tendency to be gritty. Then steam them for 7–8 minutes until tender and bright green. Toss with lemon and butter and sprinkle with 2 tsp. fresh dill, or 1 tsp. dried dill.

B.C. Asparagus is best when the stalks are dark green and firm. After rinsing, snap the stalk from the bottom; the place where it first snaps divides the tender (top) part from the tough (bottom) part. Steam thin, tender stalks for 5–6 minutes; thicker stalks will take 8–10 minutes. Squeeze lemon juice over asparagus and toss with butter.

B.C. Sugar Peas or **Snow Peas** are always a favourite. I first discovered them years ago in Chinese cuisine. These tender vegetables should be rinsed and the stems removed. They can be stir-fried for 1 minute or steamed for 2 minutes if cooked by themselves. (When I steam cauliflower and snow peas at the same time, I place the cauliflower in the lower compartment and the snow peas above them, and it takes 6–7 minutes for the steam to find its way past the cauliflower to the peas.) Toss cooked snow peas with a little butter.

B.C. Brussel Sprouts can often be found in the markets in fall attached to their huge stalks. Detach the sprout, then steam until just tender, about 6–8 minutes, depending on size. If overcooked, they are soggy and leave a heavy odour in the kitchen. Lightly steamed and tossed with fresh lemon juice and butter, they will surprise you with their delicate flavour.

Our fresh **Fennel** is a stunning side vegetable when cut into large chunks and sautéed in butter until just soft and lightly browned. Cook 6–7 minutes on medium-high heat then, just before serving, toss with 2 Tbsp. Pernod or Anisette. Tantalizing! (Pernod, incidentally, is made from fennel.) The feathery weed that tops the fennel root should be removed, but don't discard. It can be used like dill as a seasoning.

Broccoli and **Cauliflower** are both delicious when wok-fried with a little peanut oil. Just before serving, toss with 2 Tbsp. soy sauce and 1 Tbsp. sherry and sprinkle with toasted sesame seeds. (To toast sesame seeds, place in a skillet over medium heat and shake the pan, as you would when cooking popcorn, until the seeds turn brown.)

COLOURFUL RICE PILAF

3 Tbsp. butter 1 onion, chopped	Melt butter in 2-qt. saucepan and sauté onion until tender.
1/2 red bell pepper 1/2 yellow bell pepper 1/2 green bell pepper	Chop peppers and add to onion. Sauté until peppers are soft.
1 1/2 cups long grain rice	Add rice to peppers and stir until coated.
3 cups boiling water or chicken stock 1/2 tsp. salt	Add liquid and bring to a boil. Cover, reduce heat to low and simmer 18–20 minutes.
3 Tbsp. butter	Just before serving, add and toss with rice.

A tip for preventing rice from becoming mushy: *never* stir after the rice has been added to the water. *Serves 6–8.*

WILD RICE WITH RED PEPPERS & SNOW PEAS

1 cup wild rice 3 cups water 1/2 tsp. salt	Rinse rice well, drain and place in saucepan. Add water and soak rice 45 minutes. Bring to a boil, cover and simmer 40 minutes. (The rice will be just tender and will have started to split open.) Drain in sieve if necessary.
3 Tbsp. peanut oil 1 onion, chopped 1 clove garlic, chopped 1 red bell pepper, chopped	While rice is cooking, sauté vegetables and set aside.
1 Tbsp. soy sauce or Tamari 1 Tbsp. sherry	Add to cooked rice.
	Stir onion and peppers into rice.
4 oz. snow peas	Steam 30 seconds, then fold into rice.
1/4 cup cashews, toasted	Place rice in serving dish and sprinkle nuts over top.

Our Canadian wild rice is a wonderful accompaniment to any main course, particularly chicken or fish. *Serves 6.*

Restaurant Favourites

KOKO JAPANESE RESTAURANT

Koko Japanese Restaurant on East Hastings is a bit out of the way, but well worth the drive. Koko's California Roll is made with fresh Dungeness crab and you'll never find fresher sushi in Vancouver. Treat yourself to an evening of entertainment sitting at the sushi bar and watching the chefs at work, including Mr. Koji himself. Vancouverites have Mr. Koji to thank for popularizing Japanese food here long before it was the trend! Open 7 days a week.

Koko Japanese Restaurant, 2053 East Hastings Street, Vancouver, B.C. — **251–1328.**

California Roll

Rice:

3 cups sushi rice	Wash in cold water. Drain in strainer.
3 1/3 cups cold water	Combine rice and water in saucepan. Bring water to a boil, cover, reduce heat and simmer until water has been absorbed. Do not uncover for at least 20 minutes.
2 Tbsp. vinegar 1 Tbsp. sugar 1/2 tsp. salt	Heat vinegar, sugar and salt. Pour over rice and mix. Let rice cool.

(*Cont'd over*)

Photo #8: Koko's California Roll.

To Assemble:

4 sheets nori (seaweed for sushi)	Cut each sheet of nori to 2/3 its original size so that one edge is 1/3 longer. Place rice evenly on nori.
sudare (bamboo sushi mat)	Wet sudare with water.
	Put nori with rice, rice side facing down, on sudare. Place more rice 1″ wide on top of nori. Place this rice horizontally.
Japanese mayonnaise (in tube)	Squeeze mayonnaise over rice on top.
4 Tbsp. tobikko (flying fish roe)	Place tobikko on top of mayonnaise.
1 avocado, sliced	Layer one-quarter of avocado over rice on top.
8 pieces cooked crab leg (about 6 oz.)	Place crab horizontally below rice.
	Hold bottom ends of mat with fingers of both hands and roll up, lining the bottom line of mat to cover all ingredients in centre, then fold halfway up further and press well so that rice sticks together. Remove mat.
8 Tbsp. sesame seeds	Brown in skillet over medium-high heat, then press seeds over roll.

This is a delicacy not to be missed! *Makes 4 rolls.*

Koko's Teriyaki Salmon

4 – 5-oz. fillets spring or sockeye salmon

Teriyaki Sauce:

1/2 cup soy sauce 1/2 cup mirin (Japanese rice wine) 3 Tbsp. mizuame (potato or rice or millet jelly)	Combine in saucepan and bring to a boil over low heat. Remove from heat and ignite to burn off alcohol.
Light oil	Fry salmon in skillet in oil 3 minutes on each side or broil 3–5 minutes on each side.
	Pour teriyaki sauce over salmon and serve immediately.

Follow this recipe for the most authentic-tasting teriyaki sauce you've ever had. It took much coaxing to get this very simple recipe! Enjoy! *Serves 4.*

THE RESTAURANT AT MARK JAMES

The Restaurant at Mark James in Kitsilano represents the ultimate in West Coast trendsetting. Located on-site with one of the top men's, as well as women's, clothing stores, this restaurant is Vancouver's first food and fashion experience. Hats off to Mark James for bringing this concept to Vancouver — and to chef Ron Lammie for his always-changing menu! I always like to shop before I eat! Call for reservations. The Restaurant is open 7 days a week.

The Restaurant at Mark James, 2486 Bayswater Street, Vancouver, B.C. — **734–1325.**

Ron Lammie's White Chocolate Mousse

12 oz. white chocolate	Chop into small pieces and melt over hot water. Cool.
3 cups heavy cream	Whip until stiff, then refrigerate.
2 egg yolks 2 whole eggs	Beat egg yolks and whole eggs together.
3/4 cup sugar	Add sugar and beat until a light lemon colour.
1 1/2 Tbsp. unflavoured gelatine	Stir a little of the egg mixture into the gelatine, then add gelatine to eggs and mix thoroughly.
	Beat melted chocolate slowly into mixture.
	Fold in whipped cream. Place in 8-cup mould and place in refrigerator for 2 hours.

Dark Chocolate Layer:

24 oz. semi-sweet chocolate	Chop into small bits.
1 1/2 cups heavy cream 5 Tbsp. sugar 3 Tbsp. butter	Combine and bring to a boil. Remove from heat. Add chocolate and mix until blended. Cool at room temperature for 2 hours.
2 Tbsp. Grand Marnier	Add Grand Marnier. Pour over top of white chocolate mould. Refrigerate 4 hours.
	Dip mould in warm water. Turn onto serving dish.

A most coveted recipe! *Serves 8–10.*

Farfalle with Sundried Tomatoes & Prosciutto

2 oz. prosciutto 2 oz. sundried tomatoes	Using a sharp knife, slice prosciutto and tomatoes very thin (julienne style).
4 Tbsp. olive oil	Sauté prosciutto and tomatoes in oil 2–3 minutes.
1 tsp. crushed garlic	Add and toss.
1 1/2 Tbsp. chopped fresh basil 1/2 cup chicken stock	Add and simmer 2–3 minutes.
1 lb. farfalle	Cook in boiling, salted water: 5–7 minutes.
2 Tbsp. butter	Toss farfalle with above, then add butter.
Extra virgin olive oil Freshly grated Parmesan cheese	Serve farfalle in pasta bowls. Top each serving with 1 tsp. olive oil and a sprinkling of Parmesan cheese.

Sundried tomatoes have a sharp and salty taste. It's an experience you will want to repeat and repeat! *Serves 4.*

Thai Salad

1 – 15 oz. jar artichoke hearts	Cut into quarters.
1 – 14 oz. tin hearts of palm	Cut into 1″ strips.
1/4 tsp. chopped fresh ginger 1/4 tsp. crushed garlic 1/4 cup hot chili sesame oil 1/4 cup olive oil 1 red bell pepper, pureed (about 4 oz.) 1 Tbsp. chopped fresh parsley Salt and pepper to taste 1/2 tsp. Szechuan hot and sour seasoning	In food processor or blender, mix together.
	Place artichoke and palm hearts on a bed of lettuce and pour over dressing.

I forced Mark to part with these recipes. In fact, they were the inspiration for this section of the cookbook! Hot chili sesame oil and Szechuan hot and sour seasoning can be found in specialty food shops. They are worth hunting for. *Serves 4.*

THE RAGA

For the hot and spicy flavours of East Indian cuisine, The Raga is not to be missed!
From exotic curries to the hot fires of the Tandoori oven, each dish that comes out of the
kitchen at The Raga has a taste all its own. Their Indian breads are the best I've ever
had! This Restaurant is usually packed, so it's a good idea to reserve ahead. Open
7 days a week.

The Raga Restaurant, 1177 West Broadway, Vancouver, B.C. — **733–1127.**

Samosas

Pastry:

1 1/2 cups flour 3/4 tsp. salt }	Sift flour and salt into a bowl.
1 Tbsp. oil (or ghee) 1/2 cup warm water	Add oil (or ghee) and water and mix thoroughly until the ingredients are combined. Knead for about 10 minutes, until the dough is elastic. Cover with plastic wrap and set aside.

Filling:

1 Tbsp. oil (or ghee)	Heat in a saucepan.
1 clove garlic, crushed	Add and fry.
1 tsp. finely grated fresh ginger	Add and sauté.
2 medium onions, chopped	Add half the onion, reserving other half, and sauté until soft.
2 tsp. curry powder	Stir in curry.
1 Tbsp. vinegar or lemon juice 1/2 tsp. salt	Add and stir to mix.
1 lb. minced beef or lamb	Add meat and fry over high heat until meat changes colour.
1/2 cup hot water	Lower heat and add water to saucepan. Stir well and cover. Cook until meat is tender and liquid has been absorbed. Stir frequently to prevent meat from sticking to pan.
1 tsp. garam masala	Add to above.
2 Tbsp. chopped fresh mint or coriander leaves	Add, with reserved onion.

(Cont'd over)

To Assemble:

Shape small pieces of dough into balls. On a lightly floured board, roll each into very thin rounds the size of a saucer. Cut each in half. Put 1 Tbsp. of meat mixture on each half circle. Brush the edges of the dough with water. Fold dough over meat and press to make a triangular-shaped samosa.

Deep fry in oil (or ghee) until golden brown on both sides.

Samosas are East Indian hors d'oeuvres — spicy filling in a flaky pastry shell. Ghee and garam masala can be found in stores specializing in East Indian foods. *Makes 18–24 samosas.*

Pakoras

1 1/2 cups besan (chick pea flour)
1 tsp. garam masala
2 tsp. salt
1/2 tsp. ground turmeric
1/2 tsp. chili powder

Mix together in a bowl.

Gradually add enough water to make a thick batter. (It should be very thick, but still workable.)

1 clove garlic, crushed

Add garlic to batter and beat well. Let stand 30 minutes.

1/2 cup water
4 cups mixed, chopped fresh vegetables (cauliflower, potato, eggplant)

Add to batter and beat well.

Oil (or ghee) for deep frying

Heat oil (or ghee) in a deep fryer until hot, then reduce heat to moderate. Drop mixture by the teaspoon into oil and fry. When pakoras are golden on both sides, lift out with slotted spoon and drain on paper towels.

Pakoras resemble a vegetable fritter and are served as an hors d'oeuvre. They are usually made with vegetables, but fish and shrimp pakoras are fast becoming a gourmet's delight. *Serves 8.*

Eggplant Bartha

2 large eggplants, unpeeled 2 large ripe tomatoes }	Wash and dice.
3 Tbsp. oil (or ghee)	Heat oil (or ghee) in a saucepan.
2 medium onions, finely chopped 1 1/2 tsp. finely grated fresh ginger }	Fry until soft and beginning to brown.
1/2 tsp. turmeric 1/2 tsp. chili powder 2 tsp. salt 1 tsp. garam masala }	Add spices to above.

Add eggplant and tomatoes to saucepan. Stir well and cover. Reduce heat to low and cook until vegetables are soft. Stir occasionally to prevent vegetables from sticking to pan. Cook until liquid has evaporated and puree is thick and dry enough to scoop up.

This can be served as a vegetarian main course or as a vegetable side dish with a spicy meal. Serve with Indian breads. *Serves 6.*

DAR LEBANON

Dar Lebanon now has two locations on West Broadway — Dar Lebanon Restaurant and Dar Lebanon Palace — and one location downtown on Howe Street. These Middle Eastern–style restaurants feature houmos, falafel and eggplant salads, among other things. For a quick meal or fantastic take-out, you'll be impressed with their food and prices. Owners Talal and Laila El Bakkar are always on hand at the Broadway locations to answer any questions you might have about their cuisine and to make sure you enjoy yourself. Open 7 days a week.

Dar Lebanon Restaurant, 695 West Broadway, Vancouver, B.C. — **876–3636.**.
Dar Lebanon Palace, 678 West Broadway, Vancouver, B.C. — **873–9511.**
Dar Lebanon Downtown, 564 Howe Street, Vancouver, B.C. — **688–7534.**

Houmos

1 lb. dried chick peas (garbanzo beans) or 1-lb. can

Cover dried beans with water. Soak overnight. Drain, add fresh water, bring to a boil, cover and cook until soft. (If using canned beans, drain, cover with water and boil 5 minutes.)

1/3 cup Tahini
Juice of 2 lemons
Salt to taste
3 Tbsp. olive oil

Mix together in a bowl and then process with chick peas in a blender or food processor until a thick paste is formed.

Spread mixture on a flat plate and garnish with black olives, fresh parsley and paprika.

An appetizer dip. Serve with pita bread. *Serves 4.*

Baba Ganouj

Preheat oven to 500°F.

2 eggplants, unpeeled

Prick eggplants all over with a fork. Place on baking sheet and bake until tender (about 25 minutes). Split each eggplant and scoop out pulp and juices.

1/2 cup Tahini
2 Tbsp. olive oil
1 clove garlic, minced
Juice of 3 lemons

Mix together in a bowl.

Add eggplant and mix together thoroughly. Spread mixture on a flat plate and garnish with black olives and fresh parsley.

1–2 Tbsp. olive oil

Drizzle oil over top.

Tahini can be purchased in specialty food shops. Serve with pita bread. *Serves 4.*

Tabouleh

1/2 cup fine bulgar (cracked wheat)

Wash bulgar. Soak until soft (about 10 minutes). Drain and place in a bowl.

2 large tomatoes, finely diced
1/2 bunch green onions, finely chopped
6–7 bunches finely chopped fresh parsley

Add to above and mix together.

Juice of 3 lemons
1/2 cup olive oil
1 Tbsp. salt
1/2 tsp. pepper

Add to above and mix together thoroughly.

Place in refrigerator and let rest 1 hour until juices are absorbed.

Serve with pita bread as an appetizer or a side dish. *Serves 4.*

GRANDVIEW RESTAURANT

Partners Fred Jim, Howard Tang and chef Lei Cheng Lu are always ready to greet you with a smile and make sure that you are happy with the varied Chinese cuisine at this restaurant. Specialties include hot and spicy Szechuan cooking and many vegetarian dishes. The Grandview has the best egg rolls in town, and the vegetarian hot and sour soup is a must. Ask about their special seafood dishes. Be sure to call ahead for reservations. Open 7 days a week during Expo.

Grandview Restaurant, 60 West Broadway, Vancouver, B.C. — **879–8885.**

Beef with Tangerine Peel

1 lb. sirloin beef, sliced thin

Marinade:

1 Tbsp. soy sauce
2 tsp. sugar
1/4 tsp. salt
1/2 tsp. cornstarch dissolved in 1 Tbsp. water
1/2 tsp. baking soda

Mix together and toss with beef. Marinate for 20 minutes.

Sauce:

1 cup chicken stock
1 1/2 Tbsp. soy sauce
1 tsp. sugar
1/2 tsp. salt
1 1/2 Tbsp. oyster sauce
1 tsp. cornstarch dissolved in 2 Tbsp. hot water

Mix together well and set aside.

3 Tbsp. peanut oil

Heat oil in wok (or heavy skillet). Add beef and stir until just cooked (2–3 minutes). Remove beef and clean wok.

2 tsp. crushed fresh ginger
2 tsp. crushed garlic
10–12 pieces dried tangerine peel
10 Chinese green onions, cut into 1" pieces
10 pods dried red chilis, cut into pieces

Add to wok and toss over heat for 2–3 minutes.

1 tsp. oil

Add to above with beef and toss.

Pour sauce over meat and cook until thickened.

Chinese green onions can be found in Chinese produce markets. If unavailable, any variety of green onion can be substituted. *Serves 4.*

Kung Pao Chicken

1 lb. chicken, boned and diced

Marinade:

1 Tbsp. soy sauce
1 tsp. sugar
1/2 tsp. salt
1/2 tsp. cornstarch dissolved
in 1 Tbsp. water
1 tsp. oil

Mix together and toss with chicken. Marinate for 20 minutes.

Sauce:

1 cup chicken stock (or chicken bouillon)
1 Tbsp. soy sauce
1 Tbsp. vinegar
1 tsp. sugar
1 tsp. salt
1 tsp. cornstarch dissolved in
1 Tbsp. hot water

Combine thoroughly and set aside.

3–4 Tbsp. peanut oil

Heat oil in wok (or heavy skillet). Sauté chicken until tender. Remove chicken and clean wok.

2 tsp. crushed fresh ginger
2 tsp. crushed garlic
7 Chinese green onions, bottoms only, cut into 1″ pieces
10 peppercorns
10 pods dried red chilis, cut into small pieces

Add to wok and cook for 1 minute.

Add chicken and toss for 1–2 minutes.

Pour sauce over chicken and cook until thickened.

6–8 oz. unsalted peanuts

Top with peanuts.

For extra crispness, deep-fry the peanuts before adding. *Serves 4.*

ISADORA'S

Isadora's is a co-operatively-owned restaurant on Granville Island. The food is top quality; the price is great; and the atmosphere enjoyable. The adjacent waterpark and playground contribute to the fun, especially if you have kids. I also like the fact that the restaurant has a non-smoking section. John McBride graciously parted with my favourite item on their menu, the Vegetarian Nut Burger. Open 7 days a week.

Isadora's Co-operative Restaurant, 1540 Old Bridge, Granville Island, Vancouver, B.C. — **681–8816.**

Isadora's Vegetarian Nut Burgers

3 cups chopped walnuts
2 1/2 cups fine bread crumbs
1/2 cup grated carrots
1/3 cup grated Monterey Jack cheese
1/3 cup hulled sunflower seeds
4 large eggs
2 Tbsp. Tamari
2 tsp. crushed garlic
1 cup vegetable oil

Mix together thoroughly (a food processor makes this easy).

Form mixture into patties and grill, turning to brown both sides.

I crave these nut burgers regularly — and recommend them smothered with fried onions and mushrooms on a huge bun with lettuce, tomatoes and a bit of mayonnaise. *Serves 6.*

LAS MARGARITAS

Las Margaritas is another contribution to the hospitality strip on West 4th Avenue. At this restaurant, Yolande Salazar-Hobrough and her family will treat you to their brand of California-style Mexican cuisine. Open 7 days a week. Las Margaritas has a second location downtown if you can't make it to West 4th Avenue.

Las Margaritas, 1999 West 4th Avenue, Vancouver, B.C. — **734–7117.**
Las Margaritas, 745 Thurlow Street, Vancouver, B.C. — **669–5877.**

Chimichanga del Mar

Preheat oven to 400°F.

2 Tbsp. butter 1 green onion, chopped	Sauté onion in butter in saucepan 1 minute.
4 oz. fresh scallops 4 oz. fresh shrimp or prawns 4 oz. fresh salmon, cut in bite-sized pieces	Add to saucepan and cook 3 minutes.
3 sprigs fresh coriander, stems removed, finely chopped	Add to above.
2 Tbsp. chopped tinned green chilis, rinsed well and patted dry	Add to above.
2 Tbsp. sour cream	Add to above. Drain off excess liquid and set aside.
2 large flour tortillas	Soften, wrapped in foil in 325°F. oven for 5 minutes or wrapped in plastic bag in microwave for 15 seconds.
Melted butter	Evenly divide seafood mixture between 2 tortillas. Fold into tortillas like an envelope. Place, seam side down, on a lightly buttered baking sheet and brush with butter.
	Bake 15–20 minutes until golden brown. Serve immediately.

Serve with salsa (*see following recipe*) or guacamole and sour cream. *Serves 2.*

Las Margaritas Salsa

1/4 cup chopped tinned green chilis, rinsed well and patted dry
4 sprigs fresh coriander, stems removed
1/4–1/2 onion, cut in small chunks
2 very ripe tomatoes
1/4 tsp. crushed chili
1/2 tsp. salt
1 – 6-oz. tin tomato sauce (*optional*)

Combine all ingredients in a blender or food processor until preferred consistency is reached.

Nachos

1 – 6-oz. tin refried beans
1 1/2 tsp. chili powder

Combine and warm in saucepan over low heat to soften.

1 pkg. tostada shells
4 oz. cheddar cheese, grated

Spread tostada shells with beans and cover with grated cheese.

Place under broiler until cheese melts.

1/2 cup guacamole

Spread guacamole over cheese.

Sour cream

Garnish with sour cream. Cut nachos in wedges and serve.

BINKY'S OYSTER BAR & RESTAURANT

The corner of Robson and Thurlow is the hottest corner in Vancouver and tucked away in the courtyard of the Manhattan Apartments is Binky's Oyster Bar & Restaurant, where you'll find the best oysters in town! Binky's is owned by Celia Duthie and Nick Hunt, who also own Manhattan Books on Robson Street, and Duthie Books down the street near Robson Square. Binky's has a lovely courtyard in the summertime and it has a well-stocked magazine rack which is a Vancouver tradition. Grab a book at Duthie's or a newspaper at the Manhattan and relax at Binky's. They have great cappuccino! Open 7 days a week.

Binky's Oyster Bar & Restaurant, 784 Thurlow Street, Vancouver, B.C. — **681–7073.**

Binky's Oyster Croque Monsieur

Béchamel Sauce:

3 Tbsp. butter 1 clove garlic, crushed }	Melt butter in a saucepan and add garlic.
3 Tbsp. flour	Add to above, stirring constantly with a whisk.
2 1/2 cups milk	Gradually add to above, stirring constantly with a whisk until mixture is thickened.
1 tsp. dry mustard 1/2 tsp. ground thyme 1/2 tsp. ground oregano Salt and pepper to taste }	Add and set aside.

Oysters:

12 fresh oysters, shucked 1 cup white wine	Poach oysters very lightly in wine.
Salt and pepper to taste	Season with salt and pepper.
	Allow oysters to cool, then cut in half lengthwise.

To Assemble:

Preheat oven to 375°F.

12 slices fresh white or rye bread	Spread Béchamel Sauce on 6 slices of bread. Put 4 oyster halves on each bread slice.
1 1/2 cups grated Swiss cheese	Sprinkle with cheese.
	Spread Béchamel Sauce on remaining 6 slices of bread. Place these slices on top of oysters and grated cheese.
Additional grated Swiss cheese Paprika	Spread Béchamel Sauce over top of each sandwich. Sprinkle with extra grated Swiss cheese and paprika.
1 Tbsp. butter	Melt onto a 10 x 12" baking sheet. Bake sandwiches 10 minutes until brown. Serve immediately.

A rich West Coast oyster sandwich! *Serves 6.*

BISHOP'S

Bishop's has taken 4th Avenue by storm! From the day John Bishop opened, he has watched his devoted customers fill every seat in the house. With virtually no advertising, word of mouth has spread that for quality of food and fabulous prices this is a restaurant not to be missed! John Bishop is one of those all-round great guys who deserves every bit of his success. Call for reservations. Open 7 days a week during Expo.

Bishop's, 2183 West 4th Avenue, Vancouver, B.C. — **738–2025.**

Bishop's Rack of Lamb

	Preheat oven to 450°F.
1 – 2–lb. rack of lamb	Clean lamb.
1/2 tsp. honey mustard	Rub lamb with mustard.
1 sprig fresh rosemary 1 clove garlic, coarsely chopped	Sprinkle with rosemary and garlic.
Salt and freshly ground pepper to taste	Season with salt and pepper.
	Place in a lightly oiled ovenproof skillet and gently brown meat on all sides.
	Place skillet in oven and roast 15 minutes until just pink. Remove and allow to rest 5 minutes. Discard excess fat from skillet.
1/4 cup dry red wine	Swill skillet with wine. Return to heat and cook 2 minutes until reduced.
2 cups thickened veal (or beef) stock	Add to above and simmer over medium heat 5 minutes.
Salt and freshly ground pepper to taste	Season with salt and pepper.
	Carve lamb and place on heated dinner plates. Lightly coat with sauce.

Serve with vegetables of the season. *Serves 2–4.*

Photo #9: Bishop's Rack of Lamb.

LE CROCODILE

Michel Jacob and partner Roger Chrisp introduced this intimate dining experience to Vancouver in 1983. Since then, they have never looked back. Although the restaurant is always packed, each plate that is served is a masterpiece of taste and visual design. In addition, Michel is one of the nicest chefs I've ever met. Reservations are essential. Open 7 days a week during Expo.

Le Crocodile, 818 Thurlow Street, Vancouver, B.C. — **669–4298.**

Michel Jacob's Poached Pears with Raspberry Sauce & Chocolate Mousse

6 whole pears	Peel, but leave stem on. Set aside.

Syrup:

4 cups water 2 cups sugar Juice of 2 lemons, and whole rinds 1/2 vanilla bean	Combine in large saucepan. Boil 20 minutes.
	Place pears in syrup. Cover with a clean cloth. (This will keep the pears immersed while they cook.) Simmer 35–45 minutes until fruit is tender.

Raspberry Sauce:

2 cups fresh or frozen and thawed raspberries	Mash, blend or process.
1/2 cup sugar	Add to raspberries, stirring to blend. Press mixture through a sieve. Set aside.

Chocolate Mousse:

4 oz. semi-sweet chocolate	Melt over hot water. Let cool slightly.
1 cup heavy cream 3 Tbsp. sugar	Whip together until stiff peaks form.
4 egg whites	Beat until stiff peaks form.
	Fold cream into chocolate. Fold in egg whites.
3 Tbsp. coarsely chopped almonds, toasted	Mix into mousse, then chill.

(*Cont'd over*)

Photo #10: Le Crocodile's Poached Pear.

To Serve:

Place raspberry sauce on a serving plate. Drain pear and place upright on sauce. Put 2 small ovals of mousse on raspberry sauce. Garnish with a sprig of mint on each pear stem.

Voilà! *Serves 6.*

Mussels Setoise

4 doz. mussels	Scrub mussels. In a large skillet, steam until shells open. Crack off top shells and discard.
1/2 lb. soft butter 1 tsp. salt 1/2 tsp. pepper 1/4 tsp. nutmeg 2 Tbsp. tomato paste 1/4 head garlic, crushed 1 Tbsp. Pernod Juice of 1/2 lemon	In food processor or blender, process until well blended.
1/2 medium tomato	Peel, chop coarsely and add to above. Using a rubber spatula, cover each mussel with some of mixture.
1/3 cup fine bread crumbs Chopped fresh parsley	Top with crumbs and parsley.
	In ovenproof serving dishes, place mussels under broiler for 4–5 minutes.
	Serve immediately with French bread.

Everytime I eat at Le Crocodile, I start with this appetizer. (And then dream about it afterwards!) *Serves 4.*

THE LAZY GOURMET

Deborah Roitberg and I started The Lazy Gourmet on West 4th Avenue in 1979. Our emphasis has always been to introduce new food ideas to our customers, whether it be through our take-out menu or the foodstuffs we sell in the store. We often have on hand many of the gourmet food products that are used in this book. Drop by and see our stock and our store. Pick up one of our take-out menus and keep it by your phone. Picnics at the beach are a major focus during the summer months in Vancouver. Whether you want a romantic dinner for two or are planning a huge family get-together, you can count on The Lazy Gourmet to fill your picnic baskets. Or, if you are entertaining at home or have guests from out of town, phone The Lazy Gourmet to order dinner or dessert. Look for our second location at Granville Island Public Market.

The Lazy Gourmet, 2380 West 4th Avenue, Vancouver, B.C. — **734–2507.**
The Lazy Gourmet at Granville Island Public Market, Granville Island,
 Vancouver, B.C.

Picnic Favourites

Curried Chicken Salad

2 cups chopped celery
1 cup seeded and chopped
red bell pepper
1 cup seeded and chopped
green bell pepper
1 cup chopped mushrooms
1/2 cup coarsely chopped
toasted almonds
1/2 cup halved red seedless grapes
1/2 cup halved green seedless grapes
1/2 cup snow peas, lightly steamed
1/4 cup chopped fresh parsley
1/4 cup chopped red onion
2 cups cooked diced chicken

In large bowl, combine all ingredients.

Dressing:

1/2 cup soft cream cheese
1/2 cup plain yogurt
2/3 cup mayonnaise
2 tsp. curry powder
1 tsp.–1 Tbsp. honey (*to taste*)
2 dashes tabasco sauce
Salt and freshly ground pepper to taste

In separate bowl, whisk together until well blended.

Fold dressing into salad. Serve in melon halves (remove seeds) or between croissant halves.

Whole chunk tuna can be substituted for chicken. With this light meal, you can treat yourself to a fabulous dessert. *Serves 6–8.*

Marinated New Potato Salad

3 lbs. new red potatoes, scrubbed clean	Boil until just tender. Cool immediately under cold running water. Drain and toss at once with dressing.

Dressing:

1 cup light oil 1/4 cup white wine vinegar 2 Tbsp. fresh lemon juice 1 cup coarsely chopped fresh parsley 1/3 cup coarsely chopped fresh basil 1/2 cup finely chopped green onion 1/2 cup finely chopped red onion 1 tsp. Dijon mustard 1 clove garlic, crushed Salt and white pepper to taste	Combine with whisk in bowl or in blender.

The fresh basil makes this recipe unique. Serve this salad as a side dish with Delicious Sesame Baked Chicken (*see p. 48*) and be the envy of the beach crowd. *Serves 6.*

Indonesian Vermicelli Salad

1 lb. vermicelli	Cook in boiling, salted water: 10 minutes. Drain and set aside.

1 small head bok choy, coarsely chopped 1 small head sui choy, coarsely chopped 2 lbs. broccoli, cut into bite-sized pieces 1 large bunch green onions, chopped 6 oz. bean sprouts 1 bunch radishes, finely sliced	Combine in large bowl.

Dressing:

1/4 cup red wine vinegar 2 Tbsp. fresh lemon juice 1 3/4 cups light vegetable or peanut oil 2 Tbsp. soy sauce 1/2 tsp. cayenne 1 clove garlic, crushed Salt and pepper to taste Dash of Worcestershire sauce	Combine well in blender or food processor.
2/3 cup unsweetened peanut butter	Add to dressing and blend well.
	Toss vegetables and pasta with dressing.
1/2 cup cashews, toasted	Sprinkle over salad.

Serves 8–10.

ENGLISH BAY CAFE

Located on picturesque English Bay, the English Bay Cafe has a bustling atmosphere and one of the best views in town. The staff is always helpful, energetic and friendly and people have been known to drive from Seattle for a piece of their Chocolate Pecan Pie! Open 7 days a week.

English Bay Cafe, 1795 Beach Avenue, Vancouver, B.C. — **669-2225.**

Double Fudge Chocolate Cake

2 – 8″ or 9″ cake pans, buttered and floured	Preheat oven to 350°F.
2 eggs 1 cup sugar 2 Tbsp. soft butter 1 cup light oil 1/2 cup cocoa, packed 1/2 cup buttermilk 1 tsp. vanilla	In large bowl, add ingredients one at a time in this order, beating after each addition.
2 1/4 cups flour 1 1/2 tsp. baking soda 1 1/2 tsp. baking powder	In separate bowl, sift together, then add to above.
1 cup boiling water	Fold into above.
1/2 cup chocolate chips	Add to above and mix in.
	Place mixture in prepared pans. Bake for 25 minutes. Ice with Incredible Chocolate Icing.

Incredible Chocolate Icing:

1 cup soft butter 2 cups icing sugar 1 1/3 cups cocoa	Place in a blender or food processor and blend for a few seconds.
2 tsp. vanilla 1/4 cup milk 1/4 cup hot coffee	Add liquids and blend until smooth. For a thinner icing, use additional milk.

Chocolate Pecan Pie

Chocolate Pastry:

9" or 10" pie plate	Heat oven to 375°F.
1 cup flour 1/4 cup brown sugar } 3 Tbsp. cocoa	Combine in bowl.
1/2 cup cold butter	Cut into pieces. Blend into flour mixture until coarse, using pastry blender, 2 knives or a food processor.
2 Tbsp. milk 1 tsp. vanilla	Add to mixture and combine until just blended.
	Pat dough into pie plate and crimp edges.

Filling:

3 eggs	Beat well.
1 cup brown sugar	Stir into eggs.
1/3 cup melted butter } 1/2 tsp. vanilla	Stir into egg/sugar mixture.
1 cup toasted pecan halves	Spread pecans in bottom of pie shell. Pour filling over pecans.
	Bake 15 minutes, then reduce heat to 350°F. and bake an additional 30 minutes. Let cool to room temperature, then top with Fudge Glaze.

Fudge Glaze:

1 Tbsp. butter	Melt over hot water.
1 cup chocolate chips	In same pan, melt, then cool slightly.
2 Tbsp. brandy	Gently stir into butter/chocolate mixture. Spread glaze over pie.

Chocolate Pecan Pie is also available at P.J. Burgers & Sons, Vancouver, Richmond, North Vancouver and Coquitlam.

TONY ROMA'S

Michael Jackson was delighted to part with these tempting recipes. Tony Roma's specializes in ribs, but it also has the best french fries in town. It's always a lively, exciting place to be! Open 7 days a week during Expo.

Tony Roma's, 801 Pacific, Vancouver, B.C. — **669–7336.**

Honey Garlic Ribs

2 lbs. pork riblets	Chop ribs into 3/4″ pieces.
1/2 cup soy sauce 2 Tbsp. garlic powder 1/4 Tbsp. powdered ginger	Marinate ribs in soy sauce mixture for 2 hours, or overnight.
Oil for deep frying	Deep-fry ribs in hot oil until golden brown.

Honey Garlic Sauce:

1 1/2 cups honey 1 cup water 1 tsp. crushed garlic 1 Tbsp. Worcestershire sauce 1 Tbsp. tomato paste 2 drops Tabasco sauce 1/2 Tbsp. powdered ginger	Combine all ingredients in large saucepan and heat to boiling.
2 Tbsp. cornstarch 1/4 cup cold water	Dissolve cornstarch in water and add to above, mixing well.
	Add ribs to pan and heat, coating thoroughly with sauce.
	Serve on lettuce leaves.

The whole town has been waiting for this recipe! *Serves 4.*

Silk Pie

Crust:

3/4 cup graham wafer crumbs 2 Tbsp. melted butter	Mix together and press into bottom of 10″ springform pan.

Filling:

7 oz. semi-sweet chocolate	Melt chocolate in top of double boiler over hot water.
1 cup soft butter 1/2 cup sugar	Beat butter and sugar together and add to chocolate.
4 eggs	Beat eggs, one at a time, into above.
1 tsp. vanilla 2 Tbsp. brandy 2 Tbsp. Frangelica liqueur	Stir into above and pour over crust.

Topping:

1 1/2 cups heavy cream 1/4 cup sugar	Whip together until soft peaks form.
1 Tbsp. cocoa 1/2 Tbsp. unflavoured gelatine 1/4 cup water	Mix together and let stand until gelatine is softened, then heat until gelatine is totally dissolved.

Beat cocoa mixture into cream.

Spread over filling and refrigerate 1–2 hours until set.

Called Silk Pie because of its smooth texture.

THE CANNERY SEAFOOD RESTAURANT

The Cannery Seafood Restaurant is a Vancouver tradition. Owned by restaurateur, Bud Kanke, it is located on the waterfront on Vancouver's Eastside. Just ask a cabby to take you there, or phone for instructions if you are driving. There's plenty of parking; the staff is always friendly; and the food is consistently good! Or try Bud Kanke's other two restaurants: Mulvaney's on Granville Island or Joe Fortes on Thurlow Street. The Cannery is open 7 days a week.

The Cannery Seafood Restaurant, 2205 Commissioner Street, Vancouver, B.C.
— **254–9606.**

Mussels Cannery

1 1/2 lbs. fresh mussels	Scrub thoroughly.
1 Tbsp. oil	In large skillet, heat oil.
1/3 cup dry white wine	Add mussels and wine to skillet. Cover and steam just until mussels open.
1 oz. prosciutto, diced 1 Tbsp. lemon grass Pinch of saffron	Add to skillet.
3 Tbsp. heavy cream 2 Tbsp. butter	Add to above and cook until liquid is reduced and sauce is thick.
Salt and pepper	Season to taste.

Mussels are fast becoming a West Coast favourite. Lemon grass can be found in the herb section of markets in summer. If unavailable, substitute 1/2 tsp. fresh lemon rind. *Serves 2 as a main course and 4 as an appetizer.*

Clams in Black Bean Sauce

1 1/2 lbs. fresh clams	Scrub well.
1 Tbsp. black beans 1 clove garlic, crushed 1 tsp. grated fresh ginger 2 tsp. oil	Blend well in blender or food processor.
1 Tbsp. oil	In large skillet, heat oil until it smokes.
1 tsp. diced onion	Brown onions in oil, then add black bean mixture.
4 strips red bell pepper 4 strips green bell pepper	Add peppers to skillet.
	Add clams to skillet. Cover, uncover and stir, then cover again. (This hastens cooking time.)
1 tsp. honey 1 Tbsp. soy sauce 1 Tbsp. dry white wine 1/2 tsp. cornstarch dissolved in 2 tsp. cold water	Combine and add as soon as clams open.
White pepper	Add a pinch of pepper and stir until clams are coated with sauce.
1 tsp. oil	Add to give clams a shine.
3 sprigs fresh coriander	Garnish with coriander and serve.

A wonderful combination of West Coast ingredients and Chinese cooking technique. Black beans can be purchased in specialty food shops. *Serves 2 as a main course and 4 as an appetizer.*

Sweets & Treats

TRIPLE BERRY CRISP PIE

9″ deep-dish pie crust, prebaked
7–9 minutes at 375°F

Preheat oven to 375°F.

1 cup strawberries
2 cups raspberries
3 cups blueberries
(berries may be fresh or frozen)
1 cup sugar
3 Tbsp. cornstarch
1/4 tsp. nutmeg

Mix together in large bowl. Pour into baked pie crust.

Topping:

3/4 cup flour
1 cup brown sugar
1/2 cup quick-cooking oats
1/2 cup cold butter

Rub together to form crumbs.

Spread topping over berries. Place pie on cookie sheet (to catch runover juice) and bake 40 minutes.

Our photographer Derik Murray's favourite pie! Because this recipe is also good with frozen fruit, it's a year-round favourite.

LUSCIOUS LEMON TORTE

2 – 9″ springform pans, buttered and floured

Preheat oven to 350° F.

Sponge Cake:

6 egg whites
1/4 cup plus 2 Tbsp. sugar

Beat egg whites until soft peaks form. Gradually add sugar and beat until stiff peaks form.

6 egg yolks
1/4 cup plus 2 Tbsp. sugar

In separate bowl, beat yolks until light. Gradually add sugar and beat.

Gently fold egg whites into yolks.

1 cup plus 2 Tbsp. flour
1 1/2 tsp. baking powder

Sift together, then gently fold into above.

Pour into prepared pans and bake 35 minutes. When cool, split each layer in half horizontally.

Luscious Lemon Curd:

1 1/4 cups sugar
3/4 cup freshly squeezed lemon juice
4 whole eggs
4 egg yolks
1 1/2 Tbsp. finely grated lemon peel

Whisk together in top of double boiler over simmering water until mixture thickens (coats the back of a spoon).

14 Tbsp. soft, unsalted butter

Gradually whisk in butter, 1 Tbsp. at a time. When completely incorporated, transfer to a glass bowl. Cool at room temperature, then chill. (Can be refrigerated up to 2 weeks.)

Lemon Buttercream Icing:

1 1/2 cups soft, unsalted butter

Cream butter.

3 3/4 cups icing sugar

Gradually add until blended.

2 egg yolks

Add.

3 Tbsp. Cointreau
3 Tbsp. lemon juice
1 1/2 tsp. lemonade concentrate
(*optional*)

Combine and add to above.

To Assemble:

Layer cake with curd as filling. Ice sides and top with Lemon Buttercream and decorate with lemon slices and/or fresh berries.

This is a very tall cake and must be cut with a large knife with a serrated edge. It's one of the best desserts I know, especially when served with fresh strawberries or raspberries.

HAZELNUT TORTE WITH WHITE & DARK CHOCOLATE

3 – 9″ round baking pans	Preheat oven to 350° F.

No Flour Torte:

7 oz. chocolate chips 2 cups hazelnuts, toasted 1 1/4 cups sugar	Process in food processor until finely minced.
1 Tbsp. baking powder Pinch of salt	Add to above.
7 egg yolks 1/2 cup unsalted butter 1 Tbsp. vanilla	Add to above and process until smooth.
8 egg whites	Fold into mixture. Pour into baking pans and bake 25 minutes.

White Chocolate Ganache:

1/3 cup heavy cream	Heat slowly until very hot.
4 oz. white chocolate, broken into small chunks	Add to cream and beat vigorously until blended.
	Chill, then whip until thick.

Dark Chocolate Ganache:

1/2 cup heavy cream	Heat slowly until hot.
6 oz. semi-sweet chocolate, broken into small pieces	Add to cream, mixing vigorously until well blended.
	Chill, then whip until thick.

Lazy Gourmet Glaze:

1/4 cup butter 4 oz. semi-sweet chocolate	Melt together over hot (*not* boiling) water.
2 Tbsp. heavy cream 1 Tbsp. brandy	Mix well and add to chocolate.

To Assemble:

Place one cake on plate. Spread with 1/2 of chocolate ganache. Top with another cake. Spread with white chocolate ganache. Top with third cake. Ice sides with remaining chocolate ganache. Cover with Lazy Gourmet Glaze.

Rich, rich, rich! This recipe is best made a day ahead and refrigerated to let flavours and textures combine.

MARIE-LORE'S DACQUOISE

Preheat oven to 250°F.

6 egg whites, at room temperature Dash of salt 1/4 tsp. cream of tartar 1 tsp. vanilla	Beat together until soft peaks form.
1 cup sugar	Gradually add sugar, 1 Tbsp. at a time.
1 1/2 cups ground toasted hazelnuts or almonds 4 1/2 tsp. cornstarch	Mix nuts and cornstarch and fold into egg white mixture, in thirds, until blended.

Spread on a 10" × 12" baking sheet covered with wax paper. Bake 1 1/2 hours until crisp. Turn off heat and leave in oven another 1/2 hour.

Cut into thirds. Spread layers with Buttercream and chill until firm.

Buttercream:

6 egg yolks 6 Tbsp. sugar 2 tsp. vanilla	Place in food processor or blender and blend for 10 seconds.
2 cups soft unsalted butter	Keep machine running and gradually add softened butter.
1/4 cup unsweetened cocoa 2 tsp. instant coffee 2 Tbsp. coffee liqueur	Add to Buttercream, mixing until smooth.
2 Tbsp. icing sugar 1 cup heavy cream, whipped	To garnish, sprinkle icing sugar over top of cake. Spread cream over sides.
1/2 cup sliced toasted almonds	Press nuts into cream.

Once there was a Vancouver restaurant called Lili La Puce which made the most fabulous torte in the world. When Marie-Lore Rhodes generously gave me this recipe and I made it for my friends, they were convinced that I had resurrected a memory. This torte is for lovers of the ultimate in gastronomic treats!

TRIPLE-LAYER RASPBERRY TRUFFLE TORTE

3 – 8″ or 9″ round cake pans, buttered and floured

Preheat oven to 350°F.

Chocolate Genoise:

6 eggs — Beat 8–10 minutes until very light and fluffy.

1 cup sugar
1 tsp. vanilla } — Add very gradually, beating on high.

1/2 cup flour
1/2 cup cocoa } — Sift a little at a time over eggs and gently fold in.

10 Tbsp. butter, melted and slightly cooled — Add, 2 Tbsp. at a time, folding in very gently.

Gently pour mixture into pans, dividing equally.

Bake 10–15 minutes, or until top springs back when touched lightly.

Syrup with Framboise:

3/4 cup sugar
1 cup cold water } — Combine in saucepan. Bring to a boil and continue to boil 5 minutes. Remove from stove.

1/3 cup framboise — When syrup reaches room temperature, add framboise. Prick cake layers and gently pour syrup over each.

Crème Ganache:

2 cups heavy cream — Bring to a boil and remove from heat.

12 oz. semi-sweet chocolate, grated, or 12 oz. chocolate chips — Pour into cream and whisk vigorously until well blended.

1/4 cup framboise — Add liqueur. Chill. When cold, whip until smooth and thick.

Chill again, then make 12 small truffles using a pastry bag with a round tip or by forming small balls. Dust with cocoa and set aside. Set remaining Crème Ganache aside.

(*Cont'd over*)

Incredible Chocolate Icing:

1/2 cup soft butter 1 cup icing sugar 2/3 cup cocoa	Place in food processor and, using steel knife, blend for 4 seconds.
1 tsp. vanilla 2 Tbsp. milk 2 Tbsp. framboise	Add to above and blend until smooth. (Additional milk will make a thinner icing.)
1 1/2–2 cups fresh raspberries	Reserve some raspberries for decoration.

To Assemble:

Spread one genoise layer with half the remaining ganache and carefully press in half the raspberries. Do the same with second layer and carefully place it on top of first. Top with third layer and spread with icing.

Decorate with cocoa-dusted truffles and remaining raspberries.

Photo #11: Triple-Layer Raspberry Truffle Torte (*in foreground*) and Ron Lammie's White Chocolate Mousse from The Restaurant at Mark James (*in background*).

L.G. BARS

9″ square pan, buttered

Layer One:

1/2 cup butter
1/4 cup sugar
1 egg
1 tsp. vanilla

Mix together, then set over boiling water. Stir until slightly thickened.

2 cups vanilla wafer crumbs
or graham wafer crumbs
1 cup dessicated coconut
1/2 cup chopped hazelnuts, toasted

Combine and add to above.

Press mixture into prepared pan, pressing down to spread evenly. Let stand 15 minutes.

Layer Two:

1/4 cup soft butter
2 Tbsp. milk
2 1/2 cups icing sugar
2 tsp. instant coffee, dissolved in
2 Tbsp. hot coffee
1/4 cup cocoa

Mix well and spread over Layer One. Refrigerate 15 minutes.

Layer Three:

6 oz. white chocolate

Melt over hot (not boiling) water, then gently spread over Layer Two.

Chill until just set. Cut into squares and go crazy!

L.G. stands for Lazy Gourmet, where this new confection was invented. If you are shy of sweets, stay away!

Photo #12 (*from left to right in tray*): Red and Green Mint Nanaimo Bars, Traditional Nanaimo Bars, and Mocha Nanaimo Bars.

LAZY GOURMET MOCHA NANAIMO BARS

9" square pan, buttered

Layer One:

1/2 cup butter
1/4 cup sugar
1 egg
1 tsp. vanilla
2 Tbsp. cocoa

Mix together and set over boiling water. Stir until slightly thickened.

2 cups graham wafer crumbs
1 cup long-threaded coconut
1/2 cup chopped walnuts or pecans

Add to above.

Press mixture into prepared pan, pressing down to spread evenly. Let stand 15 minutes.

Layer Two:

1/4 cup soft butter
2 Tbsp. milk
2 cups icing sugar
2 tsp. instant coffee dissolved in
2 Tbsp. hot coffee
2 Tbsp. custard powder
1 tsp. Kahlua (*optional*)

Mix well together and spread over Layer One.

Layer Three:

5 oz. semi-sweet chocolate

Melt chocolate over hot (not boiling) water.

1 Tbsp. butter

Very slowly stir in butter. Spread over Layer Two.

Refrigerate, then cut into squares.

Nanaimo Bars were first sold commercially at The Lazy Gourmet. Now, they can be purchased all across Canada. (But sometimes we get together and reminisce about the days before N.B.'s.)

NANAIMO BAR VARIATIONS

**Traditional Nanaimo Bars
Substitute for Layer Two:**

1/4 cup soft butter
3 Tbsp. milk
2 cups icing sugar
2 Tbsp. custard powder

Mix well together and spread over Layer One.

**Mint Nanaimo Bars
Substitute for Layer Two:**

1/4 cup soft butter
3 Tbsp. milk
2 cups icing sugar
2 Tbsp. custard powder
1/2 tsp. mint extract

Mix together.

A few drops of red or green food colouring

Add to above and spread over Layer One.

TRIPLE CHUNK COOKIES

Cookie sheet, lightly buttered

Preheat oven to 375°F.

3/4 cup soft butter
1/2 cup white sugar
1/2 cup brown sugar
1 egg
1 tsp. vanilla

Cream butter. Add white sugar and beat well, then add brown sugar and beat well. Beat in egg and vanilla.

1 1/4 cups flour
1 tsp. baking powder

Sift together and add to above.

5 oz. chocolate chunks
5 oz. white chocolate chunks
1/2 cup very coarsely chopped pecans

Fold in chocolate and nuts.

Drop by spoonfuls onto prepared cookie sheet.

Bake 12–15 minutes until golden brown.

To Make Chocolate Chunks:

5 oz. semi-sweet chocolate
5 oz. white chocolate

Melt dark and white chocolate separately in double boiler over hot water. Pour onto wax paper-lined cookie sheet and chill until set.

Cut into large chunks and chill until firm.

Chips are out, chunks are here to stay!

FESTIVE SHERRY TRIFLE

Don't be put off by the number of steps in this recipe. It's really easy and fun to make, perfect for special occasions. You will need:

Sponge Cake	Raspberry jam or	Small can mandarin
Crème Patissière	preserves	oranges, drained
Whipped Cream	Small can pineapple	Small can peaches, drained
3/4 – 1 cup sherry	chunks, drained	1 kiwi (or other) fruit

Sponge Cake:

Jeliy roll pan, lined with wax paper   Preheat oven to 375° F.

3/4 cup flour
1 tsp. baking powder } Sift together and set aside.
Dash of salt

4 egg whites   Beat egg whites until soft peaks form.
1/2 cup sugar   Gradually add sugar and beat until stiff peaks form. Set aside.

4 egg yolks   Beat yolks until thick, then gradually add
1/4 cup sugar   sugar.

1 tsp. vanilla }
1 Tbsp. water } Add to yolks and beat.

Gently fold egg whites into yolks.

Sift flour mixture, 1/3 at a time, over egg mixture, folding in gently with rubber spatula.

Spread batter in prepared pan and bake 18–20 minutes. When cool, break into pieces.

Easy Crème Patissière:

1 egg yolk }
1 whole egg } Beat together in heavy stainless steel
1/4 cup sugar } saucepan.

3 Tbsp. flour   Add to above and whisk together.
Pinch of salt

2 tsp. unflavoured gelatine   Add gelatine and whisk.

1 cup milk   In separate saucepan, heat milk until very hot. Put egg mixture on heat and very gradually add hot milk, beating vigorously with whisk until thick. Do not boil. Let cool.

1 cup heavy cream
1 Tbsp. Cointreau

Whip until soft peaks form. When crème is cool and almost set, fold in. Refrigerate until ready to assemble.

Whipped Cream:

4 cups heavy cream
1/3–1/2 cup icing sugar
2 tsp. vanilla

Whip together until soft peaks form.

To Assemble:

Layer ingredients in a 4-qt. trifle bowl as follows: whipped cream; fruit pieces; pieces of cake; a sprinkling of sherry. Repeat, decorating sides of bowl with fruit.

Add a layer of raspberry jam, making sure it touches sides of bowl.

Add a layer of Crème Patissière, a layer of cake pieces sprinkled with sherry, a layer of whipped cream and a layer of fruit. Continue layering until all ingredients are used. Reserve enough whipped cream for a thick topping. Decorate with kiwi fruit or any other fresh fruit.

Makes 16 cups of dessert or enough to serve 15–20.

LAZY GOURMET CARROT CAKE WITH CREAM CHEESE ICING

Bundt pan, buttered and floured	Preheat oven to 350° F.
4 eggs	Beat until very frothy.
2 cups sugar 1 1/4 cups oil	Gradually add to eggs, beating until light.
2 cups flour 2 tsp. baking powder 1 tsp. baking soda 1 Tbsp. cinnamon 1/4 tsp. nutmeg 1/8 tsp. cloves 1/2 tsp. salt	Sift together and add to above.
2 cups grated carrots 1 cup crushed pineapple, well drained 1 tsp. vanilla 1/2 cup chopped walnuts	Combine, add to above and mix thoroughly.
	Pour into prepared pan and bake 50 minutes to 1 hour.

Cream Cheese Icing:

6 oz. cream cheese	Beat until smooth.
1/4 cup melted butter	Stir in slowly.
2 cups icing sugar 1 tsp. lemon juice 1/2 tsp. vanilla	Add and beat until smooth.

Vancouverites are using this recipe to make unique wedding cakes.

DOUBLE CHOCOLATE FRANGELICO CHEESECAKE

10″ springform pan — Preheat oven to 350°F.

Chocolate Crumb Crust:

2/3 box chocolate wafers, processed into crumbs
5 Tbsp. melted butter
} Mix together and press into bottom and sides of pan. Bake 6 minutes, then remove from oven.

1 lb. cream cheese
1/2 cup sugar
9 oz. semi-sweet chocolate, melted
2/3 cup sour cream
3 eggs
2 Tbsp. Frangelico liqueur
1/4 cup hazelnut butter
(or Nutella)
} Combine and beat with electric mixer on medium-high speed 5–6 minutes until light and creamy.

Pour over crust and bake 40–45 minutes until firm to the touch. Cool, then chill in refrigerator.

Cream Topping:

1 cup heavy cream
2–3 Tbsp. icing sugar
— Whip cream with sugar until thick.

2 Tbsp. Frangelico liqueur — Add liqueur.

Spread over cake.

If you can find a good Belgian hazelnut fondant called Guiandua, top the cake with curls of this fabulous treat. (A vegetable peeler does the trick.)

Breads & Muffins

EASY BANANA-WALNUT MUFFINS

Muffin tin, buttered, or use paper liners

Preheat oven to 400°F.

2 cups flour
1 1/2 tsp. baking soda }

Sift together.

3 eggs
3/4 cup oil
1 1/4 cups sugar
3 ripe bananas, mashed
1/2 cup chopped walnuts

Combine thoroughly, then add flour mixture and stir until just blended.

Fill muffin tin 2/3 full. Bake 20 minutes.

RASPBERRY-BLUEBERRY CORNMEAL MUFFINS

Muffin tin, buttered, or use paper liners

Preheat oven to 400°F.

1 cup cornmeal
1 cup flour
1/3 cup sugar
2 tsp. baking powder
1/4 tsp. salt

Sift together in bowl.

1 cup buttermilk
6 Tbsp. melted butter
1 egg, slightly beaten

Form a well in dry ingredients and add combined liquids, stirring until just blended.

1 cup blueberries, fresh or frozen
1/2 cup raspberries, fresh or frozen

Fold in gently until just combined.

Fill muffin tin 2/3 full and bake 20–25 minutes. Serve warm.

STICKY CINNAMON BUNS

1/2 cup warm milk 1 tsp. sugar 1 pkg. dry yeast	Dissolve sugar in milk. Add yeast and let stand 10 minutes.
1 cup butter 1/2 cup sugar	Using electric mixer and large bowl, cream butter. Add sugar, creaming until smooth.
3 eggs	Add eggs one at a time, mixing well after each addition.
3/4 cup milk 1/2 tsp. salt	Add to above.
	Stir in yeast mixture.
3 cups flour	Using low speed of mixer, beat in flour until well blended.
2 cups flour	Add until dough is very stiff and you can no longer use mixer.
	Now add enough flour so that dough does not stick to your hands. Form a ball. Place dough in lightly oiled bowl, turning to coat all sides. Cover with oiled wax paper and a damp towel. Let rise in a warm place until doubled (about 2 hours). Punch down and roll out into a large rectangle.
1/2 cup butter, melted 3/4 cup sugar	Brush dough with butter.
1/4 cup cinnamon (*yes!*) 1 cup raisins	Sprinkle with sugar/cinnamon mixture and raisins.
	Roll up dough lengthwise and cut into 2″ rounds.
1/2 cup butter, melted 3/4 cup brown sugar 1/4 cup honey 1 cup walnut or pecan pieces	Mix together and spread over bottom of 2 – 9″ pans. Place rounds on top, cover with oiled wax paper and let rise 30 minutes.
	Bake 25–30 minutes at 375° F. Let sit a few minutes before inverting onto a plate.

The sticky bun of the century! *Makes 12–18.*

KITCHEN-ART CHALLAH

1 pkg. dry yeast 1 tsp. sugar 1 cup warm water	Combine thoroughly and let sit 10 minutes.
3 cups flour 1/3 cup sugar 1/2 tsp. salt	Place in food processor bowl and use on/off to process.
1 egg 1/4 cup oil	With machine running, add egg, oil and yeast mixture. Process until a ball forms (about 1 minute).
	Turn onto floured surface and knead 1 minute. Place in lightly oiled bowl, turning to coat all sides. Cover with lightly oiled wax paper and a damp towel. Let rise in a warm place 2 hours until doubled in volume. Punch down.
	Divide larger ball into 3 pieces. Knead each for a few minutes, then roll each into a rope and braid. Repeat with smaller ball. Top the larger braid with the smaller one and place on a lightly oiled baking pan. Cover with a damp towel and let rise in a warm place for 1 hour until doubled.
1 egg, beaten 3 Tbsp. sesame seeds	Brush dough with egg and sprinkle with seeds.
	Bake at 375° F for 35–40 minutes until golden brown. When done, the bottom should make a hollow sound when tapped.

A soft and sweet egg bread traditionally served on Friday evenings in Jewish homes. Your family and friends will be impressed with this beautiful, easy-to-make challah. *Makes 1 large or 2 smaller loaves.*

Acknowledgements

With thanks for all the love and support, help and assistance, I remain forever grateful to: Deborah Roitberg, my partner and friend at The Lazy Gourmet; and to all the staff at The Lazy Gourmet; to twin sister, Lynn (author of *Chicken! Chicken! Chicken!);* to Mother Roz; to sisters, Rena and Anita; to brothers, Fred, Ira and Allan; to Susie Cantor, Peter Cassidy, Barbara Cohen, Roberta Cornwall, Barbara Charko, Alison Delosky, Audrey Ellison, Peter Fairey, Verena Fox, Barbara Larabie, Larry Lillo, Marthe Love, Ron Mayers, Zonda Nellis, Marie-Lore Rhodes, Mrs. Robinson, Marilyn Sacks, Michiko Sakata, Barbara Saliken, Cedric Smith, Lyla Solomon, Ron Stern and Lorene Vickberg; to Rob Scott, Perry Zavitz, Michael Morissette and Nancy Riesco Marchand at Derik Murray's studio; to all the wonderful restaurateurs in Vancouver who parted with their recipes for this book — with special thanks to Mr. Koji, John Bishop, Michel Jacob and Ron Lammie, whose creations we photographed; and to all the wonderful customers of The Lazy Gourmet who tested many of the recipes in this book.

To Derik Murray. Derik's photographs speak for themselves. Each image is a work of art. Derik takes a photograph as if it were being entered into a world-class competition and he makes everybody look good! His work has earned him a national client base and his photographs have swept photography awards from the New York Art Direction Award to national and regional honours. It has been a great pleasure and privilege to work with Derik once again and to experience his extraordinary style.

To Becky Paris Turner, food stylist extraordinaire. Becky's work includes recipe development and food design for editorial and advertising photography. She also works extensively in TV commercial production as a food and props stylist. Becky is a true artist of great integrity. She also has chuzpah and a great sense of humour. I'd be afraid to do a cookbook without her.

To David Robinson, who invented the cookbook in these parts and who published my first cookbook, *Mama Never Cooked Like This,* while at Talonbooks, in addition to *The Umberto Menghi Cookbook,* either of which is owned by one–tenth of the population hereabouts. David now packages cookbooks for Whitecap Books. His books include: *British Columbia Heritage Cookbook, Umberto's Pasta Book, Chicken! Chicken! Chicken!* by Lynn Mendelson; and *Summer Delights* — cooking with fresh herbs — and *Vancouver Entertains* — a menu cookbook for entertaining — written by Larissa Hooley and his mother, Josephine Robinson, who's been threatening to publish a cookbook ever since the success of *Mama Never Cooked Like This.*

PHOTO CREDITS

Cover: spacesuit by NASA (Johnson Space Centre, Houston, Texas); scarf by Zonda Nellis; hair by Sonny Off Broadway; make–up by Roger Gariepy for Avantgarde.

Food Photographs:

Food supplied by J. B. Hoy Produce, 2171 West 41st Avenue, Vancouver, B.C. (fresh produce); Forster's Fine Cheeses, 2104 West 41st Avenue, Vancouver, B.C. (specialty cheeses and biscuits); and Longliner Seafoods, Granville Island Public Market, Granville Island, Vancouver, B.C. (all the seafood).

Props Co-ordinator for Derik Murray Photography Inc.: Rob Scott.

Gravlax shot: glass star from Chachkas Design Ltd.; fork from Murchie's Tea & Coffee Ltd.

Picnic shot: blanket from Down N' Under Bedding Shops Ltd.; cutlery from Finn Ware Sales Ltd.; bottle in basket from Ikea; plastic containers from W. H. Puddifoot Ltd.; basket from Djawa Pacific Enterprises Ltd.; beer from Granville Island Brewing Co. Ltd.

Salad shot: plates from Basic Stock Cookware Ltd.

Pizza shot: plate from Mikasa; columns, head and ball from Chachkas Design Ltd.

West Coast salmon shot: Indian artifacts from Tradewind Antiques; wood surface from Folk Art Enterprises.

Halibut shot: platters from Mikasa; knife and fork from Presents of Mind.

West Coast paella shot: wood surface from Folk Art Enterprises.

California Roll shot from Koko Japanese Restaurant: terraced surface from Chachkas Design Ltd.; chopsticks from Kaya Kaya.

Rack of lamb shot from Bishop's: plate from Presents of Mind; slate surface from Quadra Stone Co. Ltd.

Poached pear shot from Le Crocodile: marble from Quadra Stone Co. Ltd.

Dessert shot from The Lazy Gourmet (*foreground*) and The Restaurant at Mark James (*background*): black and white surface from Chachkas Design Ltd.; servers from Roomers Gift Design Ltd.

Nanaimo Bars shot from The Lazy Gourmet: hors d' oeuvre tray and coffee set from Presents of Mind; granite surface from J. B. Newall Memorials.

Landscape Photographs:

Expo Centre gate by day: Jürgen Vogt; Expo Centre gate at night: Vlado Matisic; looking back to Expo Centre from B.C. Pavilion: Gunter Marx. All landscape photos of Expo courtesy of Photo/Graphics Stock Library, 1086 West 3rd Street, North Vancouver, B.C. V7P 3J6

Index

A

Asparagus
  to cook, *73*
  with Raspberry Mousseline, *30*
Artichoke Hearts. **See** Hearts of Palm
  Thai Salad
Avocado and Chicken Casserole, *71*

B

Baba Ganouj, *85*
Banana-Walnut Muffins, *120*
Barbecued Salmon. **See** Salmon
Barbecue Sauce. **See** Ribs
BARS
  Lazy Gourmet Mocha Nanaimo, *114*
  L.G., *113*
  Nanaimo Variations, *115*
BEEF
  Bourgignon, *67*
  Stroganoff, *66*
  with Tangerine Peel, *86*
Bocconcini, *15*
BREAD
  Challah, *122*
Brie
  and Pecans in Phyllo, *12*
  Caramel Almond, *12*
  Fried, *13*
Broccoli, wok-fried, *73*
Brussel Sprouts, to cook, *73*
BUNS
  Sticky Cinnamon, *121*

C

Caesar Salad, *27*
CAKES. **See also** Tortes
  Carrot with Cream Cheese
    Icing, *118*
  Double Chocolate Frangelico
    Cheesecake, *119*
  Double Fudge Chocolate, *99*
  Sponge, *116*
California Roll (Sushi), *77–78*
Camembert-en-Croûte, *14*
CASSEROLES
  Chicken Avocado, *71*

Chicken Pesto Pasta, *71*
  Fettucccine Lasagna, *72*
  Seafood Pasta, *70*
Cauliflower
  wok-fried, *73*
Caviar Pie, *17*
Celeriac
  Salad with Apples & Pecans, *25*
Challah, *122*
Chanterelles
  in Pizza, *41*, *43*
  with Chicken, *49*
CHEESES. **See also** Bocconcini; Brie;
    Camembert; Mozzarella
  Cream Cheese with Herbs
    & Garlic, *16*
  Chèvre in Pizza, *41*
  Feta & Spinach Pie, *35*
  Four-Cheese Pizza, *41*
  Four-Cheese Quiche with
    Red Peppers, *33*
  Roquefort-Walnut Won Tons, *20*
  Straws: Sesame, Poppy,
    Cheddar, *15*
Cheesecake
  Double Chocolate Frangelico, *119*
CHICKEN. **See also** Paella
  Apricot, Grandma Faye's, *45*
  Asian, Barbara Larabie's, *47*
  Broiled, with Peanut Sauce, *46*
  Casseroles; Chicken Avocado, *71*;
    with Pesto Pasta, *71*
  Cranberry-Orange, Lyla's, *46*
  Curried Salad, *97*
  Dijon, in Cream Sauce, *44*
  Honey-Garlic Wings, *47*
  Kiev with Sesame Seeds, *48*
  Kung Pao, *87*
  Pecan Crispy, *45*
  Sesame Baked, *48*
Chimichanga del Mar, *89*
Chocolate. **See also** Cakes
  Icing, *110*
  Mousse, *95*
    White Chocolate, *79*
  Pecan Pie, *100*
Cinnamon Buns, *121*
Clams in Black Bean Sauce, *104*

COOKIES
Triple Chunk, *115*
Cornmeal Muffins with Raspberries
& Blueberries, *120*
Crab & Spinach Quiche, *34*
Cream Cheese
Icing, *118*
Pastry, *36*
with Herbs & Garlic, *16*
Crème Patissière, *116*
Crust. **See also** Pastry
Pizza, *37*
Cucumber-Dill Sauce, *61*

D

Dacquoise, Marie-Lore's, *108*
DESSERTS
Chocolate Pecan Pie, *100*
Double Chocolate Frangelico
Cheesecake, *119*
Double Fudge Chocolate
Cake, *99*
Festive Sherry Trifle, *116*
Hazelnut Torte, *107*
Lazy Gourmet Carrot Cake, *118*
Lazy Gourmet Mocha Nanaimo
Bars, *114*
Lazy Gourmet Nanaimo Bars, *113*
Luscious Lemon Torte, *106*
Marie-Lore's Dacquoise, *108*
Nanaimo Bar Variations, *115*
Ron Lammie's White Chocolate
Mousse, *79*
Silk Pie, *102*
Triple Berry Crisp Pie, *105*
Triple Chunk Cookies, *115*
Triple-Layer Raspberry
Truffle Torte, *109*
DRESSINGS
Caesar, *27*
Mango Chutney, *26*
Pesto Vinaigrette, *28*
Raspberry Mousseline, *30*
Raspberry Vinaigrette, *31*

E

Eggplant
Baba Ganouj, *85*
Bartha, *83*
in Pizza, *42*
Ratatouille Tarts, *19*
with Red Snapper & Curry, *54*

F

Farfalle with Sundried Tomatoes
& Prosciutto, *80*
Fennel
to cook, *73*
Fettuccine Lasagna, *72*
Fiddlehead Greens
to cook, *73*
FISH
Halibut
Poached with Shrimp & Sundried
Tomatoes, *52*

Susie & Peter's Hazelnut
Lemon, *51*
with Basil & Parsley
Sauce, *51*
with Sweet Red Pepper
Sauce, *50*
Salmon
Barbecued, *62,63*
Florentine in Phyllo, *55*
Quiche, *33*
Spectacular Decorated Baked, *56*
Stuffing for, *59,60*
Teriyaki, *78*
Snapper
Pan-Fried with Pecan
Butter Sauce, *53*
with Eggplant & Curry, *54*

G

Gravlax, *20*
Green Beans
with Mustard Vinaigrette, *30*
with Raspberry Vinaigrette, *31*

H

Halibut. **See** Fish
Hearts of Palm
and Artichoke Heart with
Raspberry Vinaigrette, *31*
Thai Salad, *80*
Hollandaise, Blender, *60*
Houmos, *84*

I

ICINGS
Cream Cheese, *118*
Incredible Chocolate, *110*
Indonesian Vermicelli Salad, *98*

L

LAMB
Rack of, Bishop's *92*
Lasagna. **See** Fettuccine
Lazy Gourmet
Caviar Pie, *17*
Deep-Dish Spinach & Feta Pie, *35*
Fettuccine Lasagna, *72*
L.G. Bars, *113*
Glaze, *107*
Lox Mousse, *17*
Mocha Nanaimo Bars, *114*
Nanaimo Bars Variations, *115*
Lemon Torte, *106*
Lox Mousse, *17*

M

Mango Chutney Dressing, *26*
Mayonnaise
Lime, *61*
Mustard, *25*
Mozzarella
Bocconcini, *15*

Marinated, *16*
  with Tomatoes & Basil, *29*
MUFFINS
  Banana-Walnut, *120*
  Raspberry-Blueberry Cornmeal, *120*
Mussels
  Cannery, *103*
  Setoise, *96*
Mustard
  Dijon Chicken in Cream
    Sauce, *44*
  Honey Mustard Sauce, *63*
  Mayonnaise, *25*
  Sauce, Cooked, *62*
  Vinaigrette, *30*

N

Nachos, *90*
Nanaimo Bars
  L.G. Bars, *113*
  Lazy Gourmet Mocha, *114*
  Variations, *115*
Nut Burgers, *88*

O

Oysters
  Binky's Croque Monsieur, *91*
  Stuffing for Salmon, *59*

P

Paella, West Coast, *64*
Pakoras, *82*
PASTRY
  Cream Cheese, *36*
  No-Fail, *36*
PASTA
  Indonesian Vermicelli, *98*
  Pesto with Toasted Walnuts, *28*
  Primavera, *28*
  Spaghettini with Shrimp,
    Snow Peas & Red
      Peppers, *29*
Peppers, Bell
  in Four-Cheese Quiche, *33*
  in Pizza, *41, 43*
  in Spaghettini, *29*
  Sauce (Red Pepper), *50*
  Triple Pepper Salad, *25*
  with Halibut, *50*
  with Wild Rice, *74*
Pesto, *17*
Pilaf (Rice), *74*
PIES
  Chocolate Pecan, *100*
  Silk, *102*
  Triple Berry Crisp, *105*
PIZZA
  Crust, *37*
  Eggplant, Garlic & Tomato, *42*
  Four-Cheese, *41*
  Hot Pepper & Chanterelles, *43*
  with Scallops & Leeks, *42*
  with Sundried Tomatoes, Bell Peppers,
    Mushrooms & Chèvre, *41*
PORK. **See** Ribs

Q

QUICHES
  Crab & Spinach, *34*
  Four-Cheese with Red Pepper, *33*
  Fresh Salmon, *33*
  Lazy Gourmet Deep-Dish
    Spinach & Feta Pie, *35*
  Traditional Quiche Lorraine, *32*

R

Raspberries
  Muffins, Raspberry-Blueberry
    Cornmeal, *120*
  Mousseline, *30*
  Sauce, *95*
  Vinaigrette, *31*
Ratatouille Tarts, *19*
Red Bell Pepper Sauce, *50*
Red Snapper. **See** Fish (Snapper)
Restaurants, *77–103*
  Binky's Oyster Bar, *90–91*
  Bishop's, *92*
  The Cannery Seafood Restaurant, *103*
  Dar Lebanon, *84–85*
  English Bay Cafe, *99–100*
  Grandview, *86–87*
  Isadora's, *88*
  Koko Japanese Restaurant, *77–78*
  Las Margaritas, *89–90*
  The Lazy Gourmet, *97–98*
  Le Crocodile, *95–96*
  The Raga, *81–83*
  The Restaurant at Mark James, *79–80*
  Tony Roma's, *101–2*
RIBS (Pork)
  Honey Garlic, *101*
  with Texas-Style Barbecue
    Sauce, *69*
RICE
  Colourful Pilaf, *74*
  West Coast Paella, *64*
  Wild, with Red Peppers
    & Snow Peas, *74*

S

SALADS
  Curried Chicken, *97*
  French Potato, *23*
  Indonesian Vermicelli, *98*
  Marinated New Potato, *98*
  New Potato, *24*
  New Wave Caesar, *27*
  Spinach with Peanuts,
    Apples & Chutney, *26*
  Tamari-Ginger Marinated
    Vegetables, *24*
  Thai, *80*
  Triple Pepper with Garlic, *25*
Salmon. **See also** Gravlax; Lox Mousse
  Barbecued Teriyaki, *62*
  Barbecued with Lemon Butter
    Garlic Baste, *63*
  Florentine in Phyllo, *55*
  Koko's Teriyaki, *78*
  Quiche, *33*

Spectacular Decorated Baked, *56*
Salsa, *90*
Samosas, *81*
SAUCES
Blender Hollandaise, *60*
For Fish
Basil & Parsley, *51*
Butter Lemon Garlic Baste, *63*
Cucumber-Dill, *61*
Honey Mustard, *63*
Lime Mayonnaise, *61*
Mustard, *62*
Pecan Butter, *53*
Red Bell Pepper, *50*
Sweet Red Pepper, *50*
Teriyaki, *62*
For Ribs
Honey Garlic, *101*
Texas-Style Barbecue, *69*
Las Margaritas Salsa, *90*
Raspberry, *95*
Scallops
Coconut, *11*
Seviche, *65*
SEAFOOD. **See** Clams, Crab, Mussels,
Oysters, Scallops
Snapper. **See** Fish
Spaghettini. **See** Pasta
Spinach
Fresh Crab & Spinach
Quiche, *34*
Lazy Gourmet Deep-Dish
Spinach & Feta Pie, *35*
Salad with Peanuts, Apples
& Mango Chutney, *26*
Snow Peas
to cook, *73*
with Spaghettini, *29*
with Wild Rice, *74*
Stock (Fish), *65*
Stuffings (for Salmon), *59, 60*
Sundried Tomatoes
in Farfalle with Prosciutto, *80*
in Pizza, *41*
with Poached Halibut, *52*
Sushi, *77–78*

T

Tabouleh, *85*

Tamari-Ginger Marinade
(for vegetables), *24*
Teriyaki, Salmon, *62, 78*
Tomato
Paste, *38*
Sauce, *38*
TORTES
Hazelnut, *107*
Luscious Lemon, *106*
Marie-Lore's Dacquoise, *108*
Triple-Layer Raspberry Truffle, *109*
Trifle, Festive Sherry, *116*

V

VEAL
Breast Florentine, *68*
Easy Lemon, *69*
Scalopine al Marsala, *68*
VEGETABLES. **See also** Peppers, Bell
Asparagus, *30, 73*
Broccoli, *73*
Brussel Sprouts, *73*
Cauliflower, *73*
Eggplant, *19, 42, 54, 83, 85*
Fennel, *73*
Fiddlehead Greens, *73*
Green Beans, *30, 31*
Snow Peas, *29, 73*
Zucchini, *18*
Vegetarian Nut Burger, *88*
Vermicelli, Salad, *98*
Vinaigrettes. **See** Dressings

W

White Chocolate Mousse, *79*
Wild Rice
Stuffing for Salmon, *59*
with Red Peppers &
Snow Peas, *74*
Won Tons, Roquefort-Walnut, *20*

Z

Zucchini Sticks, Deep-Fried, *18*